Vocational A-level
Leisure and Recreation

Vocational A-level Leisure and Recreation

Julie Gibson and Ian Wood

Longman

In this book you will find helpful icons showing which Key Skills the Activities
can be used for:

 Communication

 Application of number

 Information technology

 Working with others

 Problem solving

 Improving own learning and performance

Pearson Education Limited
Edinburgh Gate
Harlow
Essex CM20 2JE, England
and Associated Companies throughout the world

ISBN 0 582 38161-4

British Library Cataloguing-in-Publication Data

A catalogue record for this book is available from the British Library.

Set by 3 in Humanist, Rotis Serif, Caslon
Produced by Pearson Education Limited
Printed in the United Kingdom by Henry Ling Ltd, at the Dorset Press,
Dorchester, Dorset

Contents

Preface

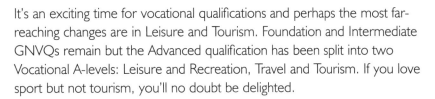

It's an exciting time for vocational qualifications and perhaps the most far-reaching changes are in Leisure and Tourism. Foundation and Intermediate GNVQs remain but the Advanced qualification has been split into two Vocational A-levels: Leisure and Recreation, Travel and Tourism. If you love sport but not tourism, you'll no doubt be delighted.

This book is for the Vocational A-level in Leisure and Recreation but Units 1, 4 and 5 may also be used for the Vocational A-level in Travel and Tourism. The text provides enough background information to get grade E under external assessment. To get grade A requires originality and creativity, evaluation and analysis.

Simple language is used throughout and important words are defined in the margins. The idea is to stimulate individual and group study in line with the philosophy of Vocational A-levels. The contents are both current and valid, based on considerable experience in industry and education. Use the book wisely and you should have an interesting programme that fills your portfolio and prepares you for assessment.

About the authors

Julie Gibson is a coordinator in vocational qualifications for Leisure and Recreation and Travel and Tourism at South East Derbyshire College. She has also worked with the awarding bodies and the Qualifications and Curriculum Authority in producing the Vocational A-level specifications. Julie is an external and internal verifier, a regular speaker on leisure and recreation, and a keen sports enthusiast.

Ian Wood works at South East Derbyshire College, where he delivers, assesses and verifies the Vocational A-level in Leisure and Recreation; he also manages the college sports facilities. Besides working with the Qualifications and Curriculum Authority to develop the compulsory units of the A-level, Ian takes part in sport as a competitor, spectator and provider.

Investigating leisure and recreation

1

Objectives

- **Be able to define leisure and recreation**
- **Understand how the industry has developed**
- **Understand how the industry is structured**
- **Be aware of the scale and impact of the industry**
- **Appreciate the employment opportunities**
- **Be able to develop strategies for progressing**

Leisure and recreation has an effect on almost everyone's life. Along with tourism, it is the one industry that continues to grow at an ever increasing rate, in the UK and worldwide. Such a diverse industry allows plenty of room for investigation. This unit will therefore explore many of the issues affecting leisure and recreation today. Starting with definitions and concluding with career opportunities, it also looks at how the industry has developed, how it is structured and the impact it is having on the UK today.

What is leisure and recreation?

Neither leisure nor recreation is easy to define. In very simplistic terms leisure refers to the *time* an individual has outside of time spent undertaking work, household chores and other essential activities such as studying, sleeping and eating. Recreation, on the other hand, refers to the type of *activities* undertaken during this time.

How people spend this free time is obviously up to them, but as will become evident later on, personal circumstances play a major part in determining the frequency and range of activities people can participate in. What will also become evident is the extensive range of products and services now available in the leisure and recreation industry.

Active recreation

During the Industrial Revolution through to the 1970s a high proportion of jobs in the UK involved manufacture or a fair degree of manual labour. Since the 1970s, however, there has been a gradual movement towards a more service-based economy in the UK, whereby people are far less physically active at work. As a consequence, active leisure pursuits – where participants expend considerable amounts of energy participating in the activity – have increased in popularity in recent years. Table 1.1 shows this increase.

Table 1.1 *Sports, games and physical activities: percentage aged 16 and over participating in each activity in the four weeks before interview*

	1987	1990	1993	1996
Walking	37.9	40.7	40.8	44.5
Swimming	13.1	14.8	15.4	14.8
Cue sports	15.1	13.6	12.2	11.3
Keep fit/yoga	8.6	11.6	12.1	12.3
Cycling	8.4	9.3	10.2	11.0
Darts	8.8	7.1	5.6	–
Weightlifting				1.3
Weightlifting/training	4.5	4.8	5.5	–
Weight training				5.6
Golf	3.9	5.0	5.3	4.7
Jogging	5.2	5.0	4.6	4.5
Football	4.8	4.6	4.5	4.8
Any activity other than walking	44.7	47.8	47.3	45.6

Source   Office for National Statistics

UNIT 1 INVESTIGATING LEISURE AND RECREATION

Bungee jumping has risen in popularity
(Courtesy of the UK Bungee Club)

There has also been an increase in popularity of activities that are out of the ordinary or potentially dangerous. One such organisation specialises in this market, appealing to the more adventurous clientele.

Passive recreation

Even though active pursuits are now in vogue, there is still a place for passive recreation. Once again, work patterns in this country have had an effect on this area of leisure. During the 1970s the UK economy was seen as the 'sick man of Europe'. It was blighted with inefficiency, poor industrial relations and falls in productivity. Since this time the UK economy has undergone a dramatic transformation and many of the previous ills are now well in the past.

Unfortunately, these changes have meant that many people now work in very intense occupations where stress and pressure are commonplace. For these people, passive pursuits such as reading or listening to music are ideal ways to wind down and forget the pressures of work. The statistics in Table 1.2 confirm the popularity of some passive recreational pursuits.

It can often be difficult to differentiate between an active pursuit and a leisure pursuit, and in many cases people enjoy a combination of the two. Likewise, much of the population split their leisure time between activities undertaken at home and those undertaken away from home.

Table 1.2 *Leisure activities: percentage aged 16 and over participating in each activity in the four weeks before interview*

	1987	1990	1993	1996
Watching TV	99	99	99	99
Visiting/entertaining friends or relatives	95	96	96	96
Listening to the radio	88	89	89	88
Listening to tapes or records	73	76	77	78
Reading books	60	62	65	65
Gardening	46	48	48	48
DIY	43	43	42	42
Dressmaking, needlework and knitting	27	23	22	22

Source Office for National Statistics

Home-based recreation

Improvements in technology have had a major impact on the home-based leisure market. Television has always been popular, but video, satellite TV and now digital TV have greatly increased the options. Other home-based recreational activities include:

- **Computers (including internet)**
- **Playstations (interactive games)**
- **Music (CDs, etc.)**
- **Gardening and DIY (encouraged by TV)**
- **Cookery (encouraged by TV)**

Away-from-home recreation

Although recreational opportunities in the home are now far enhanced, people still enjoy a traditional night out. The 1990s have seen a resurgence in many of these activities, perhaps the most startling being the growth in cinema audiences since the concept of multiplex facilities now found in most towns and cities throughout the UK. Other popular pursuits include:

- **Tenpin bowling**
- **Eating out**
- **Shopping**
- **Countryside recreation (walking, mountain biking, etc.)**

Activity
1.1

Conduct some research with your classmates or friends. Try to determine how they spend their leisure time. Take particular note of whether the activities are active or passive, home-based or away from home.

The development of leisure and recreation

Leisure and recreation has always been an important part of people's lives. Even in medieval times, when life was often hard, the population still enjoyed a certain amount of leisure time, although it was frequently linked to religious festivals and gatherings. But the most significant growth occurred during the nineteenth and twentieth centuries.

Nineteenth century

The Industrial Revolution, during the early part of the nineteenth century, saw a rapid migration of people from the countryside to the embryonic urbanised industrial areas. The lure of jobs was a great incentive for people to quit their traditional rural lifestyles, although once in the towns they were faced with terrible living and working conditions. The long and miserable hours spent in the factories made people realise how important leisure and recreation was to them.

As a consequence, many recreational pursuits grew in popularity, e.g. walking and cycling. Improvements in transport, especially the advent of the railways, allowed people to become more mobile. Day trips to the country were now possible and access to coastal resorts such as Blackpool, Scarborough and Southend saw them established as popular holiday destinations. Visits to these resorts were further accelerated by the Bank Holiday Act of 1871, which created four public holidays a year.

The mid to latter part of the century saw an explosion in organised sport. During this period football, rugby and cricket became regulated and far more structured. Participation in all sports rose to unprecedented levels and it became known as 'mass leisure'. Other activities also grew in popularity. The theatre was a popular choice, and an ever increasing number of music halls provided fun for many people.

Twentieth century

Apart from the interruptions caused by the two World Wars, leisure and recreation has grown rapidly during this century. Mobility once again has been a major influence and the increase in private car ownership has played a significant part. Car ownership has grown rapidly in this country. Numbers have more than doubled in the past 30 years, from approximately 10 million in the early 1970s to nearly 25 million today.

Although recreational activities have enjoyed a boom during this century, it has not been plain sailing for all of them. Some, such as football and the cinema, have seen major fluctuations in their popularity. Both are currently enjoying a renaissance after decidedly lean years, when attendances dropped from almost unprecedented numbers.

Activity 1.2

Research attendance figures for football matches and cinema visits during this century. Plot them on a graph and give reasons why figures may have fluctuated during this period. Can you think of any other activities that have shown similar fluctuations?

Factors affecting demand

- ✪ *Increase in leisure time*: **People, on the whole, have more leisure time in which to enjoy their favoured recreational activities. This can be explained by factors such as:**

  A shorter working week

  An increase in holiday entitlement

  More people retiring at a younger age

  Increased automation in the home

✪ *More disposable income*: **Although disposable income varies between socio-economic groups (and fluctuates with the state of the economy), it is recognised that leisure spending today is higher than it has ever been. This is as a result of:**

> Many families now having two wage earners
>
> Smaller families
>
> Improved financial advice and money management
>
> People marrying later on in life

✪ *Improved mobility*: **With a dramatic rise in car ownership, people now find it easier to participate in a range of recreational activities. Other considerations include:**

> An increase in two-car families
>
> Improved infrastructure
>
> Faster and cheaper travel (air, sea)

✪ *Changing needs and expectations*: **Society today sees leisure time as an important part of everyday life. Coupled with other changes in society, this has resulted in:**

> More interest in personal health and fitness
>
> An increase in demand for more adventure and innovation
>
> A 'work hard, play hard' attitude
>
> Joint roles within marriage

Many people have more leisure time
(Courtesy of Thorpe Park)

Leisure spending is now higher than ever
(Courtesy of the Royal Mint)

✪ *Provision*: **Taking part in recreational activity is only possible if the required facilities exist. Some recent innovations include:**

> Dry-ski slopes
>
> Free-form leisure swimming pools

Cars get people to leisure centres and hotels
(Courtesy of the Highways Agency)

Health clubs

Hi-tech bowling alleys

Activities for older clients

✪ *Demographic changes*: **The population of the UK now has what is known as an ageing population – a higher percentage of older people than ever before. This population often enjoys the greatest spending power. The increase in older people has come about through:**

People living longer due to advances in medicine

Greater health awareness

Increased affluence among the older generation

Better financial planning

Increased opportunity

The structure of the leisure and recreation industry

An industry as large and diverse as leisure and recreation invariably has a complex structure. In very broad terms, though, the industry can be divided into three types of provider: public sector, private sector and voluntary

Indoor skiing is a recent innovation
(Courtesy of Snow Dome Ski Centre)

The UK now has an ageing population
(Courtesy of the Saga Group)

sector. The public sector contains a range of organisations and facilities funded predominantly by central or local government. For ease of understanding, the two levels of public provision will be looked at separately.

Central government provision

Background

Central government, often known as the state, is an organised political structure with powers to run the affairs of the country. The government is chosen at a general election (which must be held at least once every five years), when the population over the age of 18 has the opportunity to vote for a representative from their area (constituency) to represent them in Parliament.

The majority of these representatives or members of parliament (MPs) have an allegiance to one of the main political parties (Labour, Conservative or Liberal Democrat). The political party with the majority of MPs is then empowered to form the government. The government is led by the prime minister, usually the party leader of the majority party.

The elected MPs sit in the House of Commons and their primary function is to enact legislation (make law) and to sanction the spending of public revenue. During this process they can be required to answer questions posed by the opposition – MPs representing other political parties. One of the best-known question and answer sessions is Prime Minister's Question Time, shown live on television.

Activity 1.3

Parliament consists of a lower house (the Commons) and an upper house (the Lords). Find out what role the Lords play in the government and also how it has been affected by recent changes in legislation.

The government has several departments and each one has a variety of responsibilities. These departments are run by a minister and are supported by government employees known as civil servants; civil servants are non-political. Each minister is also part of the cabinet. The cabinet is the heart of the government and it takes important decisions on policy.

Funding

Running a country does not come cheap. Central government expenditure exceeds over £250 billion per annum. It therefore requires considerable income in order to fund its various roles and responsibilities. Its main source of revenue is taxation. There are many kinds of taxation but here are the main ones:

- ✪ **Taxation of earned income (wages and salaries)**
- ✪ **Taxes on profits (corporation tax levied on the profits of companies)**

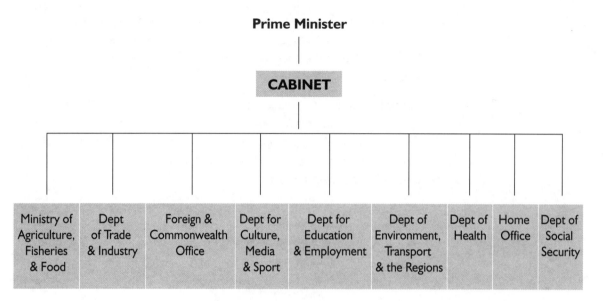

Prime Minister

CABINET

Ministry of Agriculture, Fisheries & Food	Dept of Trade & Industry	Foreign & Commonwealth Office	Dept for Culture, Media & Sport	Dept for Education & Employment	Dept of Environment, Transport & the Regions	Dept of Health	Home Office	Dept of Social Security

Cabinet ministers run government departments

- ✪ **Inheritance tax (levied on death duties, etc.)**
- ✪ **Capital gains tax (assets sold for profit, i.e. stocks and shares)**
- ✪ **Indirect taxation:**

    value added tax (VAT)

    customs and excise duties

    licences (TV, road tax, etc.)

In recent years the government coffers have been substantially improved by the sale of nationalised industries (privatisation). These industries have included:

- ✪ **Gas**
- ✪ **Telecoms**
- ✪ **Water**
- ✪ **Rail**

Influence

The government department with responsibility for leisure and recreation is the Department for Culture, Media and Sport, established in July 1997. Formerly known as the Department of National Heritage, its additional responsibilities include government policy relating to the arts, broadcasting, the press, museums and galleries, libraries, historic buildings and tourism. The current Secretary of State is the Rt Hon. Chris Smith MP. The overall aim of the department is to improve the quality of life for all through cultural and sporting activities, and to strengthen the creative industries.

With regard to sport and recreation, the Department for Culture, Media and Sport has a major influence. It funds UK Sport (formerly the UK Sports Council) and Sport England (formerly the English Sports Council), which in turn provide considerable grant aid to sports governing bodies and local government. Sport England also has the responsibility for the distribution of sport's share of the National Lottery, with plans to expand this remit to UK Sport. During the year 1999/2000 Sport England was estimated to receive £4.5 million from the government, with UK Sport receiving in excess of £12 million.

THE NATIONAL LOTTERY®

National Lottery funds go to sport and the arts
(Courtesy of Camelot Group plc)

Activity 1.4

The Department for Culture, Media and Sport has responsibilities for coordinating the government's approach to the millennium celebrations. Investigate their involvement in such projects as:

★ The Millennium Experience
★ The Dome at Greenwich
★ The Millennium Awards

Summary

Central government plays an important part in the provision of leisure and recreation in the UK. As a major funding agency and policy-making body, the government will continue to be an integral player in the leisure and recreation industry.

Local government provision

Background

Local government is carried out by local authorities, and local authorities operate at three levels:

- ✪ **County councils**
- ✪ **District or borough councils**
- ✪ **Parish councils**

Local authorities exist to provide services to their local population. Certain services are provided at county level, such as education and social services, whereas others, such as housing and leisure, are provided at borough level. Sometimes large authorities are responsible for delivering *all* the services and are known as unitary authorities.

Local authorities are operated by two distinct groups of individuals, similar to the MPs and civil servants in central government. The elected representatives, or councillors, tend to represent political parties and are elected to office every three years. Their work is unpaid (although they do receive allowances for travel, etc.) and their main responsibility is to determine the authority's policies. Due to the diverse nature of local authorities, the council's work is split between a range of committees. Each committee reports to the full council, who in turn implement the aims and objectives of the authority.

Each local authority appoints officers, paid employees with responsibility for the day-to-day running of the departments they oversee. The most senior officer at the council is the chief executive, who coordinates the work of the other officers. Each department also employs a range of staff to carry out the functions within its remit. Officers are appointed for their expertise in a certain area and they advise councillors on a range of issues. It is the councillors who ultimately make the decisions.

A recent example of this was the application by Derby County Football Club to build its Soccer Academy on greenbelt land at the outskirts of the city. The land fell within the boundaries of Erewash Borough Council, who initially rejected the application. After the club modified their plans, the officers of the council (with specific responsibility for planning) recommended that they should be accepted. However, the councillors still deemed the project unsuitable for the area and they refused the modified application.

Funding

Local government receives revenue from three main sources:

- ✪ **Grants from central government**

- ✪ **Council tax (business and residential)**
- ✪ **Charges for services provided**

With an outlay of over £1 billion annually on sport and active recreation, local authorities commit a considerable amount of their income to leisure and recreation. However, as this provision is discretionary and not a statutory duty, cutbacks are often made in this area when finances are tight or under pressure from central government.

Influence

Many local authorities provide an extensive range of recreational facilities and services, but apart from library provision, they are under no legal obligation to do this. A typical authority will provide many of these services:

- ✪ **Leisure centres**
- ✪ **Swimming pools**
- ✪ **Parks and gardens**
- ✪ **Museums**
- ✪ **Outdoor activity centres**

Summary

Local government has considerable influence on leisure and recreation; here are some facts and figures:

Shipley Country Park

Shipley Country Park is a beautiful expanse of land situated between the towns of Ilkeston and Heanor in the south-east part of Derbyshire. Managed and maintained by Derbyshire County Council, it provides a peaceful and tranquil haven for visitors. Here are some of its many services:

- ★ Walking
- ★ Cycling
- ★ Fishing
- ★ Information

- ★ Nature club
- ★ Fitness track
- ★ Cafe
- ★ Guided tours

A park of this nature is costly to maintain, staff and operate. Expenditure figures for the year 1999/2000 anticipate an outlay of £575 000 with income levels at approximately £66 000. These figures show how facilities like this consume a large amount of a local authority budget.

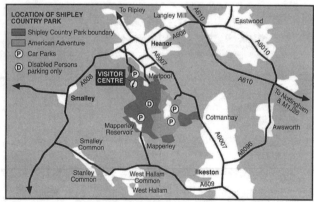

The map above details access to the Country Park. The Visitor Centre is situated at the north-western corner of the Park and is best approached from the Derby Road (A608) between Heanor and Smalley. The Country Park is well sign-posted from Heanor and the M1 motorway, Junction 26.

Access to car parks is made from either Heanor or Mapperley village. Toilets are provided at the Visitor Centre, Osborne's Pond, Derby Lodge and Mapperley car park. Much of the Country Park is accessible to all, using a network of surfaced paths and bridleways. A car park for disabled persons is provided on Shipley Hill.

At the Visitor Centre facilities include:
- ● Countryside Gift Shop and Information Centre.
  1 Apr-31 Oct 11.00-4.30pm midweek,
   10.00-6.00pm weekends.
  1 Nov-29 Feb 11.00-4.00pm midweek,
   10.00-4.30pm weekends.
  March   11.00-4.30pm midweek,
   10.00-4.30pm weekends.
- ● Exhibitions, Ramblers Coffee Shop, Function Room (available for booking) and public telephone.
- ● The Visitor Centre telephone number is (01773) 719961.
- ● Ramblers Coffee Shop can be contacted directly on (01773) 530309.

Designed & produced by Derbyshire County Council, Environmental Services Department, County Hall, Matlock, Derbyshire DE4 3AG.
Printed on recycled paper

Shipley Country Park is managed by Derbyshire County Council
(Courtesy of Derbyshire County Council Countryside Service)

- **It employs over 400 000 people nationally in leisure and recreation**
- **It runs well over 1300 leisure centres throughout the UK**
- **It owns approximately 1200 swimming pools**
- **It is instrumental in delivering sport development initiatives throughout the country**

Private sector provision

Private sector organisations fall into four categories: **sole trader**, **partnership**, **private limited company** and **public limited company**.

The public sector adopts the philosophy of 'not for profit' service provision, whereas the private sector tends to place profit maximisation above anything else. Unless profits outweigh costs, private sector leisure and recreation organisations cannot function and they will go out of business. Private sector organisations therefore involve themselves in enterprises where there is a very realistic chance of making a profit. Typical private sector facilities include:

- **Health clubs**
- **Restaurants**
- **Pubs and nightclubs**
- **Golf courses**
- **Cinemas**
- **Retail facilities**

Private sector organisations fund their operation in a variety of ways; here are the most common:

- **Personal savings**
- **Bank loans**
- **Ploughed-back profits**
- **Share issues (PLCs)**
- **Extra capital from additional partners**

The very nature of business will always carry an element of risk. Private sector leisure and recreation organisations are not immune from this risk and strive to retain their competitive edge in several different ways. Many of the most successful operations place a high emphasis on customer service and respond quickly to emerging trends and fashions. They also embrace new technology and constantly provide the paying public with innovation, excitement and adventure.

▼▼▼▼▼▼▼▼▼

Sole trader
owned and run by one person; they have personal control over all aspects of the business but are personally liable for any debts incurred by the business

Partnership
owned and run with between 2 and 20 people; decision making is shared; all partners are liable for debts incurred by the business

Private limited company
owners enjoy limited liability, i.e. they are only liable up to the amount they have invested in the company; the abbreviation 'Ltd' appears after the organisation's name; shares are not offered on the stock exchange but accounts must be published annually

Public limited company
known as PLCs; investors again share the benefit of limited liability; accounts must be published annually

▲▲▲▲▲▲▲▲▲

Find a local example for each of the four private sector organisations and prepare an information sheet on each one. Include such things as:

★ Ownership
★ Number of employees
★ Products and services
★ Visitor or user figures
★ Turnover

In this way you will build up an idea about how each operates. It may be useful to compare your findings with organisations from the public sector to see if they differ in any way.

Voluntary sector provision

The importance of voluntary sector organisations to the leisure and recreation industry is often overlooked. Without the voluntary sector, many people within the UK would not enjoy the breadth of opportunity afforded to them. The voluntary sector therefore tends to supplement public and private sector provision, offering recreational opportunities in areas such as:

✪ **Minority groups (conservation, heritage, etc.)**
✪ **Clubs and societies (sports clubs, appreciation societies, etc.)**
✪ **Youth organisations (scouts, guides, etc.)**
✪ **Community groups (playschemes, etc.)**

As the name suggests, the voluntary sector relies heavily on the goodwill of enthusiasts and helpers who dedicate time and energy to the organisations they represent. In certain cases, often within large voluntary sector organisations, paid employees are required to manage the affairs and day-to-day administration. An example of this is the National Trust. The National Trust is a large charitable organisation which relies on many unpaid volunteers but it also employs a large number of salaried staff.

Smaller organisations, such as a local squash club, would probably rely on the players to run everything. It might have a chairperson, a secretary and a treasurer. Whether small or large, all organisations need some level of finance to survive. Finance can be obtained in many ways; here are the most popular:

- ✪ **Grants from the public sector**
- ✪ **Fund-raising activities**
- ✪ **Sponsorship**
- ✪ **Playing fees**
- ✪ **Membership subscriptions**
- ✪ **Legacies and donations**

Activity 1.8

You have probably been, or still are, a member of a voluntary sector recreation organisation. It's a fair bet, though, that you will have little or no understanding of how it operates or is managed. Make a few enquiries – there might be a role for you somewhere. And if not, at least you will have a better knowledge of the effort it takes to run a club or society.

Belper Meadows Sports Club

The Belper Meadows Sports Club originated from humble beginnings in 1857, when an influential mill owner by the name of Strutt donated land to the local cricket club. In 1908 a hockey club was established, soon to be followed by a tennis and bowls club. Each club was independent until 1960 when E.D. Litchfield, a keen cricket and hockey enthusiast, formed the Belper Meadows Sports Club to encompass all four sports within one organisation.

Each section still has its own committee to run its own internal affairs, but the club has an overarching committee with representatives from each section. Every member pays an annual subscription of £38 and additional section supplements; here are the supplements for the 1998/99 season:

continued

continued

Hockey	*£39*
Cricket	*£12*
Ladies' hockey	*£27*
Bowls	*free*
Tennis	*£32*

The club has approximately 300 members and fields competitive teams in hockey (regional level) and cricket (county level). The hockey club have recently invested in a water-based AstroTurf pitch (at a cost of £400 000), funded through a lottery grant, grant aid from the local authority and the Foundation for Sports and the Arts, and extensive fund-raising activities by the members.

The club is run totally by volunteers apart from a paid part-time groundsman. In the past 25 years the hockey club has had only five chairpersons, an indication of their commitment to the club. As with any voluntary organisation, finance is a major consideration. In the year 1997/98 the hockey section made a loss of £700 despite raising over £14 500 during the season. However, with the commitment and enthusiasm of the club members, and an embryonic junior section, the future of the club is in good hands.

Changes in provision

Historically, the public and private sectors have always worked independently of each other, whereas the voluntary sector has always relied on support from the other two. However, in recent years there has been a shift towards more cooperation between the public sector and the private sector. An excellent example is compulsory competitive tendering (CCT), introduced by the Conservative government in the early 1990s. Under CCT many recreational activities within the public sector had to be opened up to tender. In essence this gave private sector organisations the opportunity to run public sector services and facilities, and the government's intention was to obtain better value from the council tax people paid.

Although many private organisations were successful in their bids, many local authorities won the tenders themselves. This had the desired effect of turning somewhat inefficient leisure departments into more businesslike and effective bodies. The Derby and Sandiacre Canal Trust provides a good example of cooperation between the three sectors.

Derby and Sandiacre Canal Trust

The Derby and Sandiacre Canal Trust, a voluntary organisation, was set up in the mid 1990s with the intention of restoring a 12 mile (19 km) section of a run-down canal. The project is expected to cost up to £30 million to complete and when finished is expected to create an estimated 3000 jobs and generate close to £7 million each year. A project of this magnitude would be impossible for a voluntary organisation to finance. The trust therefore sought private and public sector financial support, and to date they have been successful in attracting funding from both.

Private sector support came from Railtrack in the form of a £500 000 donation, thought to be the first example of a railway company helping to rebuild a canal. Other private sector involvement has included the donation of earth-moving machinery (from a building company) and smaller donations from a range of organisations. Public sector backing has included financial support (totalling £500 000) from Derby City Council, Erewash Borough Council and possible grant aid from the National Lottery Heritage Committee.

Components of the industry

With an industry as diverse as leisure and recreation, it helps to divide it into categories or component parts. Even though many of the providers are interrelated, they do have distinctive characteristics which are worth investigating. As will become clear, though, it is often difficult to pigeon-hole a particular facility or organisation into one discrete component. Bearing this in mind, here are the six key components we will look at:

- ✪ **Arts and entertainment**
- ✪ **Sport and physical recreation**

- ✪ **Heritage**
- ✪ **Catering**
- ✪ **Countryside recreation**
- ✪ **Home-based recreation**

Arts and entertainment is probably the largest of the six components and contains a multitude of organisations and facilities. Various dictionary definitions describe the word *entertainment* as 'for amusement' or 'to occupy agreeably'. If this is the case then *all* recreational providers could fall within this area; but as five other categories exist, the major players are outlined below.

Arts

The arts in the UK are currently enjoying a resurgence in popularity, mainly due to a proactive approach by the industry itself and through targeting by the government (in the form of policy and funding). An excellent example is the reopened Royal Opera House in Covent Garden, London. Much of the £214 million spent on refurbishment has come from National Lottery funding, on the

The Royal Opera House in Covent Garden, London
(Copyright Rob Moore)

premise that a traditionally elitist and expensive form of entertainment should be made more affordable and accessible to all.

Museums have also changed their image. Gone are the days when they were seen as dull and austere, full of interesting facts but often uninspiring. Many museums today have embraced high technology in order to present information in an interactive and hands-on way, allowing visitors to discover new and interesting knowledge in a fun and enjoyable environment. Other arts facilities include:

- ✪ **Dance and media studios**
- ✪ **Art galleries**
- ✪ **Theatres**
- ✪ **Cinemas**

The theatre sector of the arts is currently going through a mixed period. The major shows in London still attract vast audiences, although many of the smaller theatres in the capital are reporting drops in attendance. However, many provincial theatres are enjoying larger audience figures, attributed to an improvement in the productions but also to an increase in the products and services they provide, including:

- ✪ **Backstage tours**
- ✪ **Education days**
- ✪ **Drama workshops**
- ✪ **Sign language**
- ✪ **Audio descriptions**
- ✪ **Better food and drink**
- ✪ **Chats with the cast**
- ✪ **Open days**

Entertainment

Entertainment facilities tend to be the preserve of the private sector and generate considerable income for their owners. The biggest growth in recent years has seen leisure or theme parks increase in popularity. The most famous of them all, Disneyland, continues to attract visitors from all over the globe. Its sister park, Eurodisney, situated just outside Paris, has recovered from a troublesome beginning to become a major attraction.

The UK has also seen an upsurge of leisure parks. Many, such as Alton Towers, Thorpe Park and the Chessington World of Adventure, have been around for some time. To maintain or enhance their appeal, they have invested millions of pounds in new and exciting rides and extensive marketing campaigns. Others, such as the American Adventure theme park and Legoland, are relatively new

Legoland has proved popular with all age groups
(Courtesy of Legoland)

on the scene but they still prove popular with all age groups. Other examples of entertainment facilities include:

- **Casinos**
- **Nightclubs**
- **Public houses**
- **Bingo halls**
- **Concert venues**

The licensing trade in the UK has faced many threats over the past few years (cheap imports, availability through supermarkets, etc.) and has had to adapt to survive. Many public houses now rely heavily on income provided by food sales, whereas others have responded to the popularity of theme pubs such as Irish bars and sports bars. Others have introduced quiz and karaoke nights to attract customers. Here are some more changes and innovations:

- **Production and sale of real ales**
- **Extended opening hours**
- **Continental-style bars**
- **Non-smoking and noise-free areas**

Sports

It is estimated that 65% of the adult population (16+) participate in at least one sporting activity in any four-week period. This requires a major sports infrastructure. All three sectors contribute to sports provision. The government encourages participation in sport through grant aid and awareness campaigns, and local government provides the bulk of the facilities. The private sector, on the other hand, invests vast amounts of money in providing sporting and health-related facilities for an increasing number of the population who take their health and fitness very seriously. The voluntary sector provides the opportunity for many people to be involved in sports clubs and associated activities. Here are examples of some facilities:

- ✪ **Major spectating arenas**
- ✪ **Health and fitness clubs**
- ✪ **Sports fields**
- ✪ **Leisure centres**
- ✪ **Golf courses**
- ✪ **Outdoor sports (canoeing, cycling, etc.)**

As with the other components of the industry, facilities for sport and physical activity have undergone major changes in the past few years. Nowhere has this been more evident than in the transformation of old, dilapidated football grounds into state-of-the-art stadia. This change has been mirrored in other sports such as rugby union, where magnificent buildings like Twickenham and the Millennium Stadium in Cardiff are now evident. Many UK facilities are now the envy of the world.

But it hasn't all been plain sailing. The recent fiasco concerning the Wembley Stadium development threatens to jeopardise England's bid for the 2006 Football World Cup and any possible bid for the Olympic Games in 2012. The Wembley case study highlights some of the problems.

Wembley Stadium

Back in 1995 there was a duel between Wembley and Manchester to receive the new national stadium. In 1996 Wembley got the vote and a new facility was promised to replace the current structure, now decaying and antiquated. At that time a bid for the 2006 World Cup was not mentioned, but the Olympic Games and the World Athletics

continued

continued

The new Wembley may one day look like this
(Courtesy of Wembley National Stadium Ltd)

Championships were discussed, and considerable facilities for athletics were included in the bidding document.

It was anticipated that the cost of the new Wembley would be £220 million, £120 million of which would come from the National Lottery. The shortfall would be raised through commercial sources. It was intended that ownership of the stadium would eventually rest with the English National Stadium Trust; the trust would purchase Wembley from its then owners, Wembley plc. Negotiations, however, did not run smoothly and by the time an agreement was made in April 1998, the redevelopment costs had risen to £475 million – a massive increase on initial estimates.

During the negotiations other sports such as rugby league and football were consulted, but at no time were the British Olympic Association (BOA) involved, even though they would be instrumental in any future Olympic bids. At this stage it was evident that considerable additional finance would need to be raised from the private sector; realistically, only football was in a position to generate the

continued

continued

sums involved. A new plan was formulated with football being the dominant force. A company called Wembley National Stadium Limited (a subsidiary of the Football Association) was now put in charge of the project.

Since July 1999 the whole project has been put in doubt over protracted wrangles between the BOA, UK Sport, Sport England and Wembley National Stadium Limited. Kate Hoey, the minister for sport, is still trying to resolve the situation, although it looks as though what was intended to be a national multi-use sports stadium may become only a national football stadium.

Activity
1.9

What sports facilities are available for you in the area where you live? Conduct a quick audit. Classify them into public sector or private sector, playing and spectating or playing only. Once complete, compare your findings with other members of your group who live in different areas. Is the provision similar or are there differences? Are there any inadequacies?

The UK still hosts many sporting events which have considerable exposure throughout the world. Not only do they keep the country on the sporting map, they also generate substantial income and employ significant numbers of people. Events of this nature include:

- ✪ **The Grand National Horse Race, Aintree**
- ✪ **The University Boat Race, London**
- ✪ **The FA Cup Final, London**
- ✪ **Euro '96 Football**
- ✪ **The Rugby World Cup 1999**
- ✪ **Grand Prix Motor Racing**
- ✪ **The London Marathon**

- The British Open Golf Tournament
- The Cricket World Cup 1999

The government has recognised the value of sport to the economy of the UK, and through grant aid to Sport England it has helped establish the World Class Events Programme to attract major competitions to these shores.

Heritage

Visits to heritage sites – sites with historical or cultural tradition – continue to be a popular recreational pursuit for many people. Visitors run into millions per year, and many towns and cities in the UK are partly reliant on the jobs and income they provide. Cities such as Bath, with its Georgian architecture and Roman spa, are renowned for their heritage.

London is probably the most famous city in the UK and a special favourite with foreign visitors. Not only is it the capital of England, it is also the home to many well-known landmarks. A trip to London is not complete without a visit to Buckingham Palace, Westminster Abbey, the Tower of London and the Houses of Parliament. To many people the Royal family is the epitome of British tradition, and heritage with a Royal connection continues to be a major draw.

Outside London, stately homes, historic castles, battle sites and famous monuments all attract their fair share of visitors each year. In an attempt to broaden their appeal and to increase income, many heritage sites now offer additional products and services, including:

- **Conference facilities**
- **Information services**
- **Educational packages**
- **Displays and exhibitions**

Catering

The catering component of the industry has undergone a revolution in recent years, with the UK no longer seen as a culinary disaster area. There has been an explosion of cookery programmes on TV and a huge increase in the choice of foods we can buy. Most towns can now boast a wide variety of restaurants and fast-food outlets to suit every taste. Indian, Chinese and Mexican foods are now very popular in the UK, along with all kinds of burgers and pizzas.

More recent additions to the catering scene have been theme cafes, such as Planet Hollywood and the Hard Rock Cafe, exclusive coffee shops, even cybercafes where customers can surf the internet and enjoy a drink. But what about the fish and chip shop?

Harry Ramsden's

The Harry Ramsden story begins in the West Yorkshire city of Bradford, where Harry first sold his fish and chips. When his wife suffered an illness, Harry moved into the country and opened a new shop in Guiseley, near Leeds, in 1928. This ideal location attracted people from far and wide, and

BRADFORD BULLS FORUM . . .

HENRY PAUL
and
ROBBIE PAUL

appearing

WEDNESDAY, 22nd SEPTEMBER, 1999

hosted by.....Stuart Duffy

Come along and enjoy an evening with Henry and Robbie at the Restaurant

They will be talking about any Rugby matters you wish to ask them about

Signing autographs and having photos taken

(bring a camera!!)

**Please arrive
7.00pm for 7.30pm**

**All inclusive 3 course menu
£16.50 inc. VAT (Excluding drinks)**

Rugby stars sell fish and chips for Harry Ramsden's
(Courtesy of Harry Ramsden's)

continued

continued

what was initially a small wooden hut grew into a grandiose fish and chip restaurant. Harry soon added live entertainment.

The Harry Ramsden's empire has continued to grow, even though Harry died in 1963. Today it is a public limited company and has a policy of opening restaurants both nationally and internationally. At the last count there were over 50 restaurants in the UK and as far afield as Hong Kong, Singapore and Dubai. To retain their position as market leader, the organisation are always striving for new ideas. Reputation is not always enough; sometimes it takes an innovative idea, even if the food is excellent.

Countryside

Countryside recreation is facing a challenging period. The sheer volume of people accessing the countryside is creating environmental and social problems which are proving hard to address. On the other hand, traditional country pursuits such as fox hunting are facing a different kind of pressure, perhaps even a ban.

Whatever the problems, the countryside is still a popular venue for recreational activity. Fishing is still considered to be the sport with the highest participation rate in the UK, and other established pastimes such as walking and cycling (especially mountain biking) are gaining in popularity.

The countryside is seen as the ideal location to escape the pressures of modern society, but large numbers of visitors create a constant headache for the people who live and work in rural communities. Nowhere is this problem more acute than in the Peak District National Park, one of ten special areas designated between 1951 and 1957 following the National Parks and Access to the Countryside Act 1949.

Some 19 million people live within 60 miles (96 km) of the park, which covers 555 square miles (1440 km^2) and plays host to an estimated 22 million visitors a year, many of which arrive by car for day trips and sightseeing expeditions. The narrow lanes find it hard to manage the sheer numbers of cars, leading to traffic congestion and environmental problems. Car parking is also a problem, as is the damage done to the landscape, footpaths and plant life.

To counteract some of these issues, the Peak Tourism Partnership was formed from public, private and voluntary groups with an interest in conserving the natural beauty and character of the park. Among its initiatives, the partnership has established a tourism trust to raise funds for conservation issues. Other schemes include the marketing of less popular locations within the park, attracting people away from the traditionally busy areas. Whatever happens, the challenges facing the countryside will be with us for many years to come.

Countryside recreation has not been slow to embrace change. People's thirst for adventure has produced an upsurge of demanding and exciting activities based in the countryside. They include:

- **Gorge walking**
- **Ballooning**
- **Off-road driving**
- **Bungee jumping**
- **White-water rafting**

Balloon flights usually begin in the countryside
(Courtesy of Skypower Aerial & Media Solutions)

The scale of the leisure and recreation industry

As one of the largest industries in the UK, leisure and recreation has a significant impact on the nation's economy. For the first time ever, it is reported that people now spend more money per week on leisure than on food. This section focuses on three main areas: participation trends, consumer spending and employment statistics.

Participation trends

All providers of leisure and recreation strive to increase participation rates in their particular activity. The private sector will do this for financial reasons, whereas the public and voluntary sectors are probably aiming to improve the health of the participants or their quality of life. Whatever the motive, awareness or marketing campaigns are used to attract or persuade the public to participate in a chosen activity.

Participation in sport

One of the longest-running campaigns was Sport for All, initiated by the Sports Council in 1972. The initial aim was to highlight the benefits of regular physical activity. As well as educating the public, it also stimulated the building of sports facilities, giving people the opportunity to participate. In the mid 1980s a report commissioned by the Sports Council revealed that although general participation rates had increased since the start of their campaign, there were still some groups (school-leavers, women, etc.) that had low participation rates. As a result, the Sports Council targeted these groups with individual campaigns such as:

- ✪ **50+ All to Play For (aimed at the older generation)**
- ✪ **Ever Thought of Sport? (aimed at teenagers)**
- ✪ **What's Your Sport? (aimed at women)**

More recent statistics reveal that these campaigns may be working. Participation rates for women are growing faster than for men, and the middle-aged and elderly show the greatest increase of all. Table 1.3 shows a range of participation rates.

Participation in other activities

Today's extensive range of recreational activities has led to a competitive environment within the industry. All organisations, commercial or non-

Table 1.3   *Most popular sports, games and physical activities by age and sex: the survey base was 829 people aged 16–19 and 3686 people aged 45–59; walking was included only where the walk was for pleasure and length 2 miles or longer*

Men 16–19 years old		Men 45–59 years old	
1 Walking	58%	1 Walking	52%
2 Snooker, pool, billiards	55%	=2 Snooker, pool, billiards	12%
3 Any soccer	47%	=2 Cycling	12%
4 Cycling	37%	4 Golf	10%
5 Weight training	25%	5 Any swimming	9%
6 Any swimming	18%	6 Keep fit, yoga	5%
=7 Running (jogging, etc.)	14%	7 Running (jogging, etc.)	4%
=7 Basketball	14%	=8 Weight training	3%
9 Tenpin bowling, skittles	13%	=8 Any bowls	3%
=10 Keep fit, yoga	10%	=8 Fishing	3%
=10 Tennis	10%		
=10 Weightlifting	10%		

Women 16–19 years old		Women 45–59 years old	
1 Walking	45%	1 Walking	47%
2 Keep fit, yoga	30%	=2 Keep fit, yoga	14%
3 Snooker, pool, billiards	24%	=2 Any swimming	14%
4 Any swimming	23%	4 Cycling	7%
5 Cycling	14%	=5 Weight training	2%
6 Tenpin bowling, skittles	10%	=5 Badminton	2%
7 Running (jogging, etc.)	9%	=5 Golf	2%
8 Weight training	7%	=8 Snooker, pool, billiards	1%
=9 Badminton	6%	=8 Tenpin bowling, skittles	1%
=9 Tennis	6%	=8 Running (jogging, etc.)	1%
		=8 Tennis	1%
		=8 Horse riding	1%
		=8 Any bowls	1%

Source   General Household Survey 1996

commercial, need to attract sufficient customers to survive and progress. Individual organisations will devise their own marketing strategies to retain existing customers or attract new ones. But other factors also need to be taken into account, including:

✪ **The state of the economy**

✪ **Fashion and trends**

✪ **Exposure in the media**

✪ **Success of local or national teams**

✪ **Public campaigns**

Consumer spending

Leisure and recreation now generates large amounts of income and has a big effect on the national economy. Major spectator sports now have huge yearly turnovers and the figures for other organisations continue to go from strength to strength.

Manchester United PLC

Football in the UK is enjoying a renaissance. Nowhere is this better reflected than in the figures of Manchester United PLC. Reputedly the richest club in the world in 1997, it had an annual turnover of £87.9 million, 65% higher than the previous year. Success on the pitch has undoubtedly played a part, but so has diversification into other businesses. The club has been so successful at selling shirts, posters and other items, its income from merchandising almost matches its gate receipts.

It is estimated that Premiership clubs make close to £100 million per year from the sale of replica kit, a figure undreamt of just a few years ago. Other key areas for income generation include:

★ Television receipts (terrestrial, satellite)

★ Sponsorship

★ Conferencing and hospitality

★ Other ventures (advertising, promotions, etc.)

Employment statistics

The leisure and recreation industry is labour intensive, as are most service industries. The industry's ability to create jobs is a major economic benefit to a region or country; it creates jobs in leisure and recreation, and in other sectors such as manufacturing and retailing. Although most of the jobs are in the private sector (with ever increasing numbers of self-employed people), a fair number are in the public sector.

Working in the leisure and recreation industry

Now is a good time for anyone who wants to to work in the leisure industry. Opportunities have never been greater for a rewarding career, and there are genuine promotion prospects for employees with the right skills, knowledge and attitude. Very few industries can match leisure and recreation for variety. Even within organisations there are very often a range of jobs, all with different roles and responsibilities. Here are a few possibilities:

- **Hotel, catering and conferencing**
- **Leisure centre operations**
- **Sports or leisure administration**
- **Event management and marketing**
- **Coaching**
- **Outdoor pursuits**
- **Countryside management**
- **Performing arts or cinema**

The list is endless and can't be given justice in a short textbook. It is, however, feasible to look at two contrasting organisations and investigate the career prospects they offer.

Multiplex Cinemas

The growth of multiplex cinemas has created a heavy demand for personnel. A typical cinema would offer the following positions:

- ★ Manager
- ★ Trainee manager
- ★ House managers
- ★ Cashiers
- ★ Projectionists

continued

continued

★ Catering staff

★ Programme sellers

★ Ushers

The figure on page 37 outlines the role of a house manager with the UCI cinema chain and indicates some of the competencies that are required.

David Lloyd Health & Fitness Clubs

An organisation as large as the David Lloyd Health & Fitness Clubs will need a range of employees with different skills. Its headquarters will rely heavily on employees with administrative skills and marketing or management expertise. Senior staff will be involved at strategic level, devising policy and overseeing the corporate management of the clubs throughout the country.

At an operational level, the range of employment opportunities will be more diverse. Table 1.4 shows the staff at a multi-use facility. The general roles and responsibilities would be far more than outlined here but it does give you an insight. There would also be employment opportunities at franchise operations within a centre, which could include:

★ Retail (sportswear and equipment)

★ Crèche

★ Hairdressing

★ Sports injury clinic

House Manager Competencies

Resilience
The ability to cope with the pressures inherent in undertaking their role and manage the demands being made upon them without appearing to suffer physically or mentally.

Communications/Active listening
Communicates effectively through the spoken and written word achieving a high level of mutual understanding of the point under discussion. Is able to identify the key elements of others communication and gather relevant information through effective questioning, probing and investigation.

Interpersonal Sensitivity
Sensitivity to the needs of others and an awareness of the impact of one's behaviour on others

Action Orientation
Tendency to take action to resolve problems or initiate improvements after an appropriate level of analysis and consideration

Team Leader
Ability to build and motivate a team. Prepared to contribute to team success by putting team achievement before personal objectives and adopting different team roles

Coach/people developer
Helps team members achieve their potential through coaching, counselling and training

Customer Service
Understands and acts to meet internal and external customer needs

Controlling/Delegating
A tendency to set up and maintain systems of regulation. Can take overall command of a situation, advise and enlist the help of others, ensures appropriate action and sees the situation through to the end. Tendency to maximise subordinates effectiveness and efficiency through allocation of tasks and decision making activity.

House Manager Role Definition

Overall Purpose:

To direct, co-ordinate and influence the day to day operations of the site and its resources to achieve site business objectives through the implementation of defined operational standards policies and procedures.

Role:

Operations

Schedule the activities of people and control the utilisation resources in order to achieve the completion of all appropriate operational tasks, reporting and administration.

Regularly assist and support the site team in the completion of all operational tasks, duties and responsibilities.

To implement appropriate action within the site to achieve the Company's internal operational standards and values in the following areas:

Health & safety   Booth operations
House-keeping   Customer service
Site security   Audit
Employment relations   CAPS
Facilities management   Community relations
Payroll   Performance management

Regularly monitor and review performance in the above areas and make recommendations to the District Manager, or take appropriate action to ensure site performance is to the highest possible standard.

Human Resources

Support the Regional and District succession plan by ensuring and assisting the effective recruitment, training and development of all site personnel.

Communicate Company operating policies, procedures and directives to all employees on site through regular and effective meetings.

Business Performance

Effectively plan, schedule, direct, monitor, and evaluate defined operational resources to optimise business performance in the following areas:

Concession profit per head   Stock control
Payroll costs   Cash control
Controllable operating costs

How to be a house manager at the cinema chain UCI

Table 1.4 *Staff at a multi-use facility*

Position	General roles and responsibilities
General manager	Overseeing all areas of the club's operation Recruitment and selection of staff Budgetary control and financial planning
Assistant and deputy manager(s)	Assisting manager day-to-day Deputising for manager Staff rota and training Programming
Bar and catering manager	Overseeing food and beverage outlets Ordering stock
Membership and marketing officer	Customer care initiatives Promotional activity Achieving membership targets
Membership consultants	Day-to-day membership enquiries Securing new members
Receptionists	Day-to-day enquiries Answering the phone Administration Customer liaison
Centre attendants	Supervising members Cleaning duties Setting up and taking down equipment Supervising children's activities
Fitness advisors	Gym maintenance Gym inductions Programming and advice
Coaches	Coaching sessions
Cleaning staff	General cleaning
Catering staff	Preparation and sale of food
Maintenance	Health and safety issues Repairs and maintenance

Activity
1.10

Visit a variety of leisure providers in your area and collate a list of different jobs available in each. It may open your eyes to possibilities you never knew existed.

Advantages and disadvantages

Leisure may seem a glamorous industry to work in. There are many advantages, but before you make the decision to go for it, maybe contemplate the downside.

Advantages

- ✪ **Every day can bring different tasks**
- ✪ **It may be rewarding to help people enjoy their leisure**
- ✪ **You are usually surrounded by people enjoying themselves**
- ✪ **Most organisations have clear promotion routes**
- ✪ **There are opportunities for travel or to work outdoors**
- ✪ **There are opportunities for self-employment (coaches, personal trainers, etc.)**
- ✪ **Managers and strategy planners are well paid**
- ✪ **There are many seasonal and part-time opportunities**

Disadvantages

- ✪ **The hours may be unsociable (evenings and weekends)**
- ✪ **The public are often unpredictable and difficult to deal with**
- ✪ **There are many low-paid part-time jobs**
- ✪ **Leisure and recreation is highly competitive**
- ✪ **Some jobs require extensive training and experience**
- ✪ **Many jobs are seasonal**

Overall

In many cases the advantages far outweigh the disadvantages, and as with most occupations there are always going to be a few parts of the job which are not so enjoyable. If you are still interested, the next important step is to determine whether you have the personal attributes and skills to work in the industry. It obviously depends on the career you intend to pursue, but most employers look for some basic qualities in the people they select.

Finding jobs

One thing's for sure, very few people are offered employment without actively seeking it. Even though you are probably still in education, it is never too early to put the wheels in motion for future employment.

THE 'IDEAL' LEISURE EMPLOYEES

Adaptable, fit and healthy, consistent. Works well under pressure

Enthusiastic, liking for the job, hard-worker, friendly

Smart, approachable, confident and conscientious

Good communicator, polite, excellent inter-personal skills

Good team worker but also autonomous when needed. Good initiative. Positive approach

Proficient in information technology, well organised, reliable, honest and trustworthy

The leisure industry looks for these qualities

There are numerous organisations or contact points that will be able to supply you with relevant information on career opportunities and their entry qualifications. Here are some suggestions:

- ✪ **School or college careers advisor**
- ✪ **Local authority careers service**
- ✪ **Job centres**
- ✪ **Specialist employment agencies**
- ✪ **Trade press, e.g.** *Leisure Opportunities*
- ✪ **Governing bodies**
- ✪ **Information services, e.g. ILAM**

ILAM is the Institute of Leisure and Amenity Management. Whichever combination you choose, it is important to *prepare thoroughly* for the challenges which lie ahead. An excellent starting point is to conduct a personal audit on yourself, asking some very searching questions along the way. Although this may seem unnecessary, it can help to plan your career development and give you early identification of any potential obstacles. The following questions could form the basis of your audit:

Ask searching questions in your personal audit

- ✪ **What strengths do I possess?**
- ✪ **What weaknesses do I have?**
- ✪ **What are my interests and hobbies?**
- ✪ **Am I suitable for higher education?**
- ✪ **Would I prefer to work indoors or outdoors?**
- ✪ **Do I want to work with children, adults or a combination of both?**
- ✪ **Am I prepared to travel with my work?**
- ✪ **Am I prepared to work away from home?**
- ✪ **What sector of the industry would I like to work in?**

Once these, and possibly other questions have been answered, you should be in a position to say:

- ✪ **Whether your career options are feasible**
- ✪ **How to plan your career development**

Career aims

By now you should have a good idea whether you are suited to working in the leisure industry and what sort of career you want within it. Now the hard part – actually getting the job. One of the most important things is to obtain the correct qualifications. Make sure you know exactly what is required before you start to apply for jobs. This will need planning, possibly years in advance, as qualifications cannot be gained overnight.

By taking your Vocational A-level in Leisure and Recreation you have obviously given some thought to your future career. But it may be that you need extra qualifications for the path you have chosen. Even if they are not essential, perhaps they are desirable and perhaps they will enhance your employment prospects. These could include awards in:

- ✪ **NVQs (coaching, leadership, admin)**
- ✪ **Information technology**
- ✪ **First aid and/or lifesaving awards**
- ✪ **Foreign languages**
- ✪ **Food hygiene**
- ✪ **Marketing or accountancy**
- ✪ **Health and safety qualifications**
- ✪ **Maintenance (pool plant, ice rinks)**
- ✪ **Personnel management**

Did You Know?

SPRITO
020 7388 7755
www.sprito.org.uk

Many of the above qualifications can be studied part-time or through distance learning. Advice needs to be sought from educational establishments, local training and enterprise councils (TECs) or national training organisations (NTOs) such as the Sport and Recreation Industry Training Organisation (SPRITO).

Gaining work experience

Actually securing the position you want does not depend solely on you having the correct qualifications. In addition to the application and interview stage (see pages 43–7) many organisations require potential employees to have some sort of work experience behind them. This can often be a catch-22. How can you gain work experience when you haven't got the correct qualifications, or how can you gain the qualifications if you are already in employment?

Part-time study helps if you already have a job; you can do it by day release if your employer agrees. Another way is to retrain full-time or to study for new full-time qualifications. Gaining work experience is not so easy but there are various ways to approach it. Any of the following options will enhance your employment chances. If you can show a prospective employer you have experience in more than one of them, so much the better.

- ✪ *Work experience through education*: **Although not all courses include work experience, most colleges or schools will arrange placements for you *if you ask*. You could be proactive, sort out the placement for yourself then ask the college to endorse it**
- ✪ *Part-time work (leisure)*: **Many part-time work opportunities exist for students within the leisure industry. Gaining**

qualifications such as first aid should help you secure some work in the industry

✪ *Part-time work (non-leisure)*: **It may not always be possible to find employment in the leisure industry. If this is the case, focus on other options. It would be beneficial if the job:**

> involves contact with the public
>
> has some level of responsibility
>
> involves teamwork

✪ *Voluntary work*: **Experience can always be gained through working as a volunteer in the industry. Many organisations such as youth and charity groups will be glad of the help**

✪ *Hobbies and interests*: **These are always useful, especially if you have some responsibility, e.g.**

> coaching junior members
>
> team selection or captaincy
>
> organising travel

Applying for the job

Speculative applications

You may now be studying on the right programmes, gaining experience in the correct environment, but the job you have set your heart on does not seem to be available. It could be time for you to send out a few speculative applications to show people you exist. Even if positions are not available at the present time, many organisations may keep your details on file and contact you when a vacancy does arise, if you impress them sufficiently.

A good speculative application needs to include a covering letter, explaining the reason for your application (with brief mention of your skills and experience), and a curriculum vitae (CV), containing details pertinent to the type of work you are seeking. CVs are explained on page 45.

Application forms

Many organisations now insist applicants complete an application form when applying for a job, and in many cases they require prospective candidates to apply in writing *before* an application form is even sent. If this is the case, your letter needs to be professionally presented and persuasive, containing sufficient information to convince the employer you are worth a second look.

Once the application form has been received, it is crucial that you fill it in correctly. As the newspaper article shows, many people make fundamental

Activity 1.11

Practise your letter writing skills, drafting a speculative letter for the following types of employment:

★ Leisure centre attendant

★ Sports coach

★ Marketing trainee

★ Membership consultant

★ Sports administrator

Hopefully each of your letters will look slightly different.

Thousands in for fire jobs

COUNTYWIDE: The first recruitment of firefighters in almost three years has received more than 2,600 applications for just 12 jobs.

Derbyshire Fire and Rescue Service advertised for full-time staff on March 15 and received 2,000 applica-tions in the first four days.

The advert in the Derby Evening Telegraph marked the end of a recruitment freeze which has lasted for almost three years because of a lack of funding. Starting salary for new recruits is £15,522.

The closing date for applications is noon on Monday and a shortlist will be drawn up in early April.

With each vacancy attracting so many applications, try to make yours stand out
(Courtesy the Derby Evening Telegraph 23/3/99)

mistakes when completing application forms, often excluding themselves immediately. Some applications can be complicated but they are often accompanied by explanatory notes; read them before you complete the form. Here are some common mistakes:

✪ **Wrong colour ink (black is often stipulated)**

✪ **Sections are omitted (contrary to instructions)**

✪ **CVs are sent in place of the form (contrary to instructions)**

✪ **Too much extra information (keep to the word limit)**

✪ **Closing dates are missed (make a note of the deadline)**

All can be avoided if you read the instructions carefully, plan what you are going to put down (in rough) and then give yourself sufficient time to complete the form neatly and comprehensively.

Curriculum vitae

A curriculum vitae (CV) is a summary of your previous career, usually prepared by yourself. A good CV should be clearly laid out, contain personal information (age, address, etc.), academic and non-academic qualifications, previous work experience, interests and hobbies, a personal profile and one or two people who can give you a reference. They should be adapted to suit each position you apply for and they should focus on the specific skills and experience required for the job. Pages 46 and 47 show examples of a good CV and a good letter of application. They are annotated to highlight the important points.

Preparing for the interview

Once you get to the interview, you are almost there. Do not be discouraged if initial attempts at securing an interview are unsuccessful; this may happen early on. The same applies if you get an interview but are then unsuccessful. Your ability in applying for jobs and doing well at interview will improve with practice. Look at every knock-back as a learning experience, preparing you for ultimate success.

Interviews can be a nerve-wracking experience. Just like most other things, sufficient planning can reap rewards. The old adage certainly applies: failure to plan is planning to fail. Do your preparation thoroughly, and good luck!

- ✪ **Research the organisation; find out about their products and services, recent projects, performance, etc.**
- ✪ **Make sure you have all the information and documents they require: record of achievement, qualifications, etc.**
- ✪ **Make sure you know the exact location of the interview. Have a dry run to help you get there**
- ✪ **Wear suitable clothes and get them ready the night before**
- ✪ **Make arrangements to travel the day before if the interview is a long way away**
- ✪ **Prepare suitable questions to ask at the end of your interview**

Name in bold

Should be easy
to contact Mary!

Clear headings

Pleasant to
look at!

All structured
in the same way

Includes:
– dates
– place of work
– salary
– main duties

Includes:
– qualifications
– dates
– grade(s)

Doesn't sound
arrogant

Shows what Mary
does other than
work and education

We've seen what Mary
has done, now where
she wants to go!

Full address
and details

Relationship
to candidate

Mary Freds

93 West Road
Weston
Birmingham, BE72 2AS
Phone Work: 01635 963242 Mobile: 0970 341792 Home: 01672 124682 E-mail: freds@perinet.co.uk

EXPERIENCE

September 1993–present
Chedling Borough Council
Recreation Client Officer/Assistant Leisure Centre Manager
£18,000
Core duties include:

- Sport development
- Customer liaison through corporate systems and administration
- Project management including a £1.5 million refurbishment package
- Monitoring of C.C.T. contracts
- Staff recruitment, selection and training
- Duty officer relief

August 1990–September 1993
Renbridge District Council
Recreation and Tourism Officer
£12,000
Core duties include:

- Marketing and promotion of leisure centre
- Timetabling and monitoring of the fitness suite
- Deputising for the assistant manager where necessary
- Duty officer role including safety and security of centre

EDUCATION

Loughborough University (1989)
BSc (Honours) Recreation Management, Sport Science and Physical Education
Upper second class

John Port School Derby (1986)
A levels

- English Literature A
- Home Economics A
- French B
- General Studies D

PERSONAL PROFILE

I am an ambitious lively person who enjoys a busy professional and private life.
In my leisure time I enjoy running and completed the London Marathon in
1997 raising £1500 for diabetes. I swam competitively for 12 years,
representing and captaining national, regional and local teams. I have won
seven national titles including some at masters level.
I enjoy listening to music and travelling abroad particularly to Florida.
I am seeking a rewarding and challenging role.

REFERENCES

Peter Serton	Ray Wilmot
Swimming Development Officer	Swimming Development Officer
Chedling Leisure Centre	South Charnwell Offices
Field Road	Freckwell
Chedling	Charnwellshire
Rilfordshire	FR43 5TU
CH12 4SW	
01635 963242 extension 212	01456 657844
Line manager	Swimming coach

A typical CV or resume

Looks professional	**James Booth** **National Pool Lifeguard**
Immediately attracts your attention	

76 Trigg Street
Liveringham
Liverton
LE72 2AS
01445 672617
0930 736651 (mobile)

Looks professional

Immediately attracts your attention

All details in full

30 January 2000
South Charnwell Offices
Freckwell
Charnwellshire
FR43 5TU

Dear Mrs Wigley

Re-inforce the content

Opportunities within Freckwell Leisure Complex

I spoke today with a colleague of yours regarding any opportunities you may have available in Freckwell Leisure Complex.

As you will see from my CV I am currently employed as a lifeguard/duty officer at the Hickman Sports Centre in Rilchford and I have been employed in a number of leisure facilities across the northwest of England as a pool lifeguard and duty officer.

In July of this year I am relocating to Freckwell, in September I will become an Undergraduate at Loughborough University, studying Sport Science. To supplement my studies I am seeking to secure employment as a lifeguard.

If you think there may be any opportunities for me please call.

End on a high note! — I hope to hear from you soon.

Yours sincerely

Remember to sign it! — *James Booth*

James Booth

Remember to enclose your CV! — Enc.

A typical application letter

Interview planning can reap rewards

Activity 1.12

Prepare a CV that you would be happy to use for a range of different jobs in the leisure industry. Use information technology; not only does it look more professional than a handwritten document, it is also much easier to change and adapt. Show the completed CV to your friends, parents or lecturers; they may spot ways to improve it.

Revision questions

1 What is the difference between active recreation and passive recreation?

2 What recent innovations have increased the popularity of home-based recreation?

3 List the factors that influence the demand for recreational activities.

4 Why might families today have more disposable income?

5 Briefly differentiate between central government and local government?

6 Which government department is responsible for leisure and recreation?

7 What are the sources of income for local authorities?

8 Briefly describe the difference between a private limited company and a public limited company.

9 Give examples of how the public, private and voluntary sectors can work together in providing leisure and recreation.

10 List the six components of the leisure and recreation industry.

11 List some of the products and services supplied by each component of the leisure and recreation industry.

12 Briefly summarise the advantages and disadvantages of working in leisure and recreation.

13 Where might you seek information and advice on employment opportunities in leisure and recreation?

14 Describe a speculative letter, a CV and an application form.

15 List how you might secure a career within the leisure and tourism industry.

Safe working practices

Objectives

- **Health and safety legislation and regulations**
- **How to conduct a risk assessment**
- **How to ensure a safe and secure working environment**
- **The need for security in leisure and recreation**

All employees have the right to work in a safe and secure environment. Likewise, customers participating in leisure pursuits expect every effort to have been taken to ensure their health and well-being. But recent disasters in the industry, such as Hillsborough and the Lyme Bay canoe tragedy, highlight the ever increasing need for stringent safe working practices in the leisure and recreation industry.

This unit will give you an insight into the major health and safety legislation that affects the industry as well as helping you understand the principles of risk assessment for a range of leisure activities and practices. It concludes by investigating the need for high levels of security in the leisure and recreation industry.

Health and safety: legislation and regulations

To cover all health and safety legislation in one unit would be an almost impossible task. It is possible, however, to make you aware of key pieces of legislation and address many of the important issues they contain.

Health and Safety at Work etc. Act 1974

The Health and Safety at Work etc. Act 1974 was introduced as a legislative framework to improve already existing legislation such as the Offices, Shops and Railway Premises Act 1963 and a range of other somewhat outdated acts. It covers all persons at work, employers and employees, and it provides a comprehensive range of regulations intended to ensure high standards of health and safety in the workplace. The main focus of the act is placed on employers, who have the responsibility to:

✪ **Ensure safe working practices**

✪ **Ensure safety in the workplace**

✪ **Ensure hygiene standards are good**

✪ **Provide for the welfare of employees**

✪ **Ensure fire safety**

Employers must fulfil their responsibilities under the act; employees have a duty to observe safety rules and practices. Here are the main aspects:

✪ **To take care not to endanger themselves or anyone else through their work activities**

✪ **To cooperate with their employers by following laid-down procedures and practices**

✪ **Not to interfere or misuse any equipment provided for health and safety**

Control of Substances Hazardous to Health (COSHH 2) Regulations 1994

Many leisure facilities and organisations use hazardous substances for a range of different purposes, such as water treatment in a swimming pool or

Activity

2.1

The main duties placed upon employers are listed below. Use them as the basis for an investigation into the health and safety management at a leisure and recreation facility of your choice. Contact the facility in advance and speak to someone with direct responsibility for health and safety.

★ Prepare a written statement of the organisation's health and safety policy and ensure adequate arrangements are made to carry out the policy

★ Ensure that all systems of work are safe and that they are closely monitored

★ Ensure that handling, storage, use and transport of articles and substances is performed in a safe way

★ Ensure protective clothing is supplied and used where necessary

★ Ensure there are safe means of access and exit at all times

★ Ensure there are no risks to the health and safety of customers using the organisation

★ Provide information about health and safety to all employees

★ Ensure training programmes include instruction in health and safety

★ Provide facilities for the welfare and use of employees

cleaning a large sports stadium. The COSHH Regulations ensure that the substances are used in a safe way. The 1994 regulations cover four main areas:

✪ **Acquisition and dissemination of information and knowledge about hazardous substances**

✪ **The assessment of risks to health associated with the use, handling and storage of substances at work**

✪ **Elimination or control of health risks by the use of appropriate applications, procedures and personal protection**

✪ **Monitoring the effectiveness of the measures taken**

Page 55 shows a typical COSHH information sheet. It contains important information on such things as the properties, usage and emergency procedures for the substance in question.

Reporting of Injuries, Diseases and Dangerous Occurrence Regulations 1995

These regulations cover the requirement to report certain categories of injury and disease sustained by people at work. Under normal circumstances the enforcing agency is the Health and Safety Executive (HSE); see page 61. Briefly, the regulations require injuries or dangerous occurrences (specified in the act) to be reported by the quickest possible means, followed by a written report within 10 days of:

- ✪ **The death of any person at work as the result of an accident**
- ✪ **Any person suffering a major injury (as specified) at work**
- ✪ **Any person who is not at work as a result of an injury sustained at work**
- ✪ **Where there is a dangerous occurrence at work**

Health and Safety (First Aid) Regulations 1981

This act places a general duty on employers to make, or ensure there is made, adequate first aid provision for their employees if they are injured or become ill at work. Here are some specific requirements on employers:

- ✪ **Provide equipment and facilities sufficient to enable first aid to be rendered to employees if they are injured or become ill at work**
- ✪ **Provide a sufficient number of staff trained in first aid for rendering treatment to employees who become ill or injured**

The act also gives guidance on such matters as the contents of first aid boxes, the equipment required and the recruitment and selection of first aid personnel.

Hazardous substance/COSHH assessment

Section:	03
Form	03/25
Issue no:	B
Revision no:	I

Activity/process (if applicable)	Name of substance:

Assessed by: Position:	Date of assessment: Date of review:

Name/address of supplier

Tel: **Product data sheet attached?   Y/N**

Product type	Chemicals and appearance
Hazard category (please tick) Irritant ☐ Harmful ☐ Highly flammable ☐ Toxic ☐ Corrosive ☐ Oxidising ☐	
Risks associated with use	
Control measures	
Personal protection	
Training and information	
Storage	
Fire precautions	
Disposal and spillage	

Exposure	Effect	First Aid
Skin		
Eyes		
Inhalation		
Swallowing		

Overall assessment of risk (please tick)   Low ☐   Medium ☐   High ☐

A typical COSHH information sheet
(Courtesy South East Derbyshire College)

Health and Safety at Work etc Act 1974
The Reporting of Injuries, Diseases and Dangerous Occurrences Regulations 1995

HSE Health & Safety Executive

Report of an injury or dangerous occurrence

Filling in this form
This form must be filled in by an employer or other responsible person.

Part A

About you

1 What is your full name?

2 What is your job title?

3 What is your telephone number?

About your organisation

4 What is the name of your organisation?

5 What is its address and postcode?

6 What type of work does the organisation do?

Part B

About the incident

1 On what date did the incident happen?
/ /

2 At what time did the incident happen?
(Please use the 24-hour clock eg 0600)

3 Did the incident happen at the above address?
Yes ☐ Go to question 4
No ☐ Where did the incident happen?
☐ elsewhere in your organisation – give the name, address and postcode
☐ at someone else's premises – give the name, address and postcode
☐ in a public place – give details of where it happened

If you do not know the postcode, what is the name of the local authority?

4 In which department, or where on the premises, did the incident happen?

Part C

About the injured person

If you are reporting a dangerous occurrence, go to Part F.
If more than one person was injured in the same incident, please attach the details asked for in Part C and Part D for each injured person.

1 What is their full name?

2 What is their home address and postcode?

3 What is their home phone number?

4 How old are they?

5 Are they
☐ male?
☐ female?

6 What is their job title?

7 Was the injured person (tick only one box)
☐ one of your employees?
☐ on a training scheme? Give details:

☐ on work experience?
☐ employed by someone else? Give details of the employer:

☐ self-employed and at work?
☐ a member of the public?

Part D

About the injury

1 What was the injury? (eg fracture, laceration)

2 What part of the body was injured?

3 Was the injury (tick the one box that applies)
☐ a fatality?
☐ a major injury or condition? (see accompanying notes)
☐ an injury to an employee or self-employed person which prevented them doing their normal work for more than 3 days?
☐ an injury to a member of the public which meant they had to be taken from the scene of the accident to a hospital for treatment?

4 Did the injured person (tick all the boxes that apply)
☐ become unconscious?
☐ need resuscitation?
☐ remain in hospital for more than 24 hours?
☐ none of the above.

Part E

About the kind of accident

Please tick the one box that best describes what happened, then go to Part G.
☐ Contact with moving machinery or material being machined
☐ Hit by a moving, flying or falling object
☐ Hit by a moving vehicle
☐ Hit something fixed or stationary
☐ Injured while handling, lifting or carrying
☐ Slipped, tripped or fell on the same level
☐ Fell from a height
How high was the fall? ___ metres
☐ Trapped by something collapsing
☐ Drowned or asphyxiated
☐ Exposed to, or in contact with, a harmful substance
☐ Exposed to fire
☐ Exposed to an explosion
☐ Contact with electricity or an electrical discharge
☐ Injured by an animal
☐ Physically assaulted by a person
☐ Another kind of accident (describe it in Part G)

Part F

Dangerous occurrences

Enter the number of the dangerous occurrence you are reporting. (The numbers are given in the Regulations and in the notes which accompany this form)

Part G

Describing what happened

Give as much detail as you can. For instance
• the name of any substance involved
• the name and type of any machine involved
• the events that led to the incident
• the part played by any people.

If it was a personal injury, give details of what the person was doing. Describe any action that has since been taken to prevent a similar incident. Use a separate piece of paper if you need to.

Part H

Your signature
Signature

Date / /

Where to send the form
Please send it to the Enforcing Authority for the place where it happened. If you do not know the Enforcing Authority, send it to the nearest HSE office.

For official use
Client number   Location number   Event number

☐ INV REP ☐ Y ☐ N

Some injuries require a written report
(Courtesy Health and Safety Executive)

Fire Safety and Safety of Places of Sport Act 1987

After the terrible events at Bradford City football club in 1985 (when 56 spectators lost their lives) the Popplewell Committee of Inquiry was set up to investigate the cause of the tragedy. The report gave rise to the Fire Safety and Safety of Places of Sport Act 1987, which in turn amended the Fire Precautions Act 1971, legislation principally concerning the provision of:

- **Means of escape in the event of fire**
- **The means for fighting fire**

Fire legislation applies to all premises in use for industrial, commercial or public purposes and is enforced by local fire authorities. Central to the legislation is the requirement that premises have a fire certificate which specifies:

- **The particular use of the premises it covers**
- **The means of escape in case of fire**
- **The means by which safe escape can be ensured at all times**
- **The means for fighting fire**
- **The means for giving warnings in the case of fire**
- **Information about storage and use of highly flammable liquids on the premises**

The 1987 act modified the 1971 act by reducing the need for certification for premises with a low risk, allowing fire authorities to grant exemptions in these cases. It did, however, extend the Safety of Sports Grounds Act 1975 to include all sports grounds (previously only applicable to sports stadiums). The main addition in 1987 was the need for all sports grounds to have a general safety certificate, subject to at least a yearly inspection. In addition, where a sports ground provides covered accommodation in stands for spectators (for 500 or more), a safety certificate is required for each stand (known as a regulated stand). These safety certificates are issued and enforced by local authorities.

Food Safety Act 1990

Many leisure and recreation facilities have diversified their product and service range to incorporate the sale of food. Where this is so, the Food Hygiene Regulations must be adhered to as failure to comply can result in fines or, in the worst circumstances, a ban from serving food altogether. Inspectors from the local authority will check on such things as:

- ✪ **Standards of cleanliness and hygiene**
- ✪ **Correct storage of food**
- ✪ **Correct preparation of food**

European directives

In 1993 the European Union implemented six new sets of health and safety at work regulations as part of the modernising process of current legislation and the drive towards greater European integration. The new 'six pack', as they are often affectionately known, built on or clarified existing legislation and as with the 1974 act have had a major impact on the leisure and recreation industry. The new regulations cover the following areas.

The Management of Health and Safety at Work Regulations 1992

These regulations require employers to undertake a systematic approach to health and safety management. In many ways they reflect the duties imposed by the 1974 act, although the need for employers to conduct risk assessments is a major addition. Risk assessment is covered in greater detail on page 68 but briefly requires an employer to:

- ✪ **Assess any risks to the health and safety of employees and customers**
- ✪ **Record their findings accordingly (if employing five or more people)**
- ✪ **Put into practice measures to control or eliminate risks**
- ✪ **Monitor and review measures on a regular basis**

The European Parliament in Brussels
(Courtesy the European Parliament)

The Provision and Use of Work Equipment Regulations 1992

These regulations cover equipment from small items such as hand-held microphones through to major equipment such as a swimming pool filtration system. All equipment used must conform to European safety directives and in addition:

- ✪ **Only be used for its intended purpose**
- ✪ **Be maintained on a regular basis**

Any staff using the equipment must receive adequate training and information on how to use it safely and correctly.

The Manual Handling Operations Regulations 1992

These regulations build on the risk assessment process required under the management regulation on page 58. They are designed to eliminate the numerous injuries caused annually through incorrect lifting techniques and bad practice. In brief, employers are required to:

- ✪ **Assess all manual handling operations**
- ✪ **Avoid potentially dangerous practice through ceasing altogether or by providing suitable equipment**
- ✪ **Provide staff with instruction and training on safe techniques of manual handling**

Exercise 2.1

List five manual handling operations you would consider carry an element of risk or injury potential (from a leisure and recreation scenario). What measures would you put in place to ensure the danger was eradicated or reduced?

The Workplace (Health, Safety and Welfare) Regulations 1992

These regulations require an employer to provide a safe and hygienic workplace for all employees. Here are some of the areas they cover:

Are your workers sitting comfortably? study

HEALTH inspectors are to examine workplace toilets next week after a study revealed that 10 per cent of employers provide dirty of broken facilities.

Research conducted by the Health and Safety Executive found that a significant minority of workplaces across the country failed to meet standards set by law.

From Monday, inspectors will visit sites and prosecute any employer providing facilities of an inadequate standard.

Companies can face fines of up to £5,000 if they fail to improve toilets and washing provisions which are found to be unacceptable.

"The inspectors will be looking to enforce legislation contained in several acts," said John Ewins, head of the HSE's operations in the Midlands.

"We will be targeting places such as construction sites, scrap yards, sawmills and small factories, industries which are most likely to provide facilities which are below standard."

Health and safety legislation requires all employers to provide enough flushing toilets for their workforce, toilet rolls and other sanitary provisions, coat pegs and hot running water.

"Adequate welfare facilities are a fundamental right of all employees. It is shocking that, more than 2,000 years after the introduction of piped hot water, some employers are failing to meet these basic needs," said Mr Ewins.

"In most cases, there can be no excuse for not providing proper welfare facilities. They are not expensive to provide, nor to keep in good condition.

"Simple steps, such as ensuring soap and towels are available and keeping facilities clean, may be all that is needed."

Employees still experience problems
(Courtesy the Derby Evening Telegraph 27/11/99)

- ✪ **Facilities (toilets, washrooms, rest areas, etc.)**
- ✪ **Work environment (temperature, lighting, ventilation, etc.)**
- ✪ **Hygiene (cleanliness, waste removal, etc.)**

Newspapers highlight some of the problems *still* being experienced by employees in the UK.

The Personal Protective Equipment Regulations 1992

These regulations require employers to provide, free of charge, any personal protective equipment (PPE) deemed necessary to carry out potentially hazardous tasks or operations. The equipment can range from a simple pair of gloves through to elaborate breathing apparatus. In addition to supplying suitable equipment, an employer must give training, instruction and information to staff on the correct use and care of protective equipment. Then it must:

- ✪ **Maintain and clean PPE**
- ✪ **Replace PPE when necessary**
- ✪ **Provide storage for PPE**
- ✪ **Ensure that PPE is properly used**

The Health and Safety (Display Screen Equipment) Regulations 1992

The leisure and recreation industry, like many others, has undergone a technical revolution in recent years. More and more organisations rely heavily on information technology and the Display Screen Equipment Regulations 1992 ensure employers take steps to reduce many of the muscular and mental problems associated with using visual display units (VDUs). Briefly, an employer must:

- ✪ **Provide suitable furniture for operators (adjustable chairs, etc.)**
- ✪ **Plan work so that breaks or changes in activity are possible**
- ✪ **Arrange for free eyesight tests and spectacles if required**

Enforcement of health and safety

The Health and Safety at Work etc. Act 1974 established the Health and Safety Commission (HSC), responsible to the Secretary of State for Employment. The HSC's remit is to ensure the health, safety and welfare of people at work and the well-being of the public in general. The Health and Safety Executive (HSE) enforces legislation on behalf of the HSC and has wide-ranging powers. Inspectors appointed by the HSE can enter premises at any time, either to ensure health and safety legislation is being adhered to or to investigate after accidents have occurred. Sanctions available to inspectors include:

- ✪ *Prohibition notice*: **issued to stop an activity if it is deemed hazardous or dangerous**
- ✪ *Improvement notice*: **usually issued with a time limit to rectify the problem**
- ✪ *Closure*: **if a facility or organisation poses a serious risk to employees and/or the public**

Any organisation or individual found contravening health and safety legislation could be prosecuted, leading to a fine or, for more serious offences, imprisonment. Local authorities also play a major role in enforcing health and safety legislation. Examples include:

- ✪ *Fire authorities* **issuing fire certificates under the Fire Precautions Act 1971**
- ✪ *Local authorities* **enforcing food regulations under the Food Safety Act 1990 and the registering of premises or organisations under the Children Act 1989**

Licensing and insurance

Not only do leisure and recreation facilities and organisations need to adhere to health and safety requirements, there is also a requirement to conform to a range of licensing and insurance legislation. The main licences an operator may need to consider are a **liquor licence**, **public entertainment licence**, **indoor sports licence** and **cinema licence**.

▼▼▼▼▼▼▼▼▼

Liquor licence
for premises where alcohol is sold and consumed; can range from an on-licence through to an occasional licence; applications are made to the local magistrates' court

Public entertainment licence
for premises where any form of public entertainment takes place; issued through a local authority

Indoor sports licence
required if the operator is promoting sports events to which the public are invited

Cinema licence
premises where films, videos or live events are broadcast

▲▲▲▲▲▲▲▲▲

Insurance can be defined as a contract between two parties. One, the insurer, will indemnify the other, the insured, against some form of loss. Here are the major insurance requirements:

✪ *Public liability*: **this covers visitors to a facility against injury**
✪ *Employer liability*: **insures on-duty employees in the case of injury**
✪ *Fire and property insurance*: **insures against damage to buildings and/or contents**

Applying health and safety

Having a knowledge of health and safety legislation is one thing, applying it is another. As a prospective leisure and recreation employee, applying your knowledge is crucial if events and/or facilities are to run smoothly and safely. Extensive literature is available such as the *Guide to health, safety and welfare at pop concerts and similar events*, published jointly by the HSC, the Home Office and the Scottish Office. It is an extensive guide that gives excellent practical advice on a range of issues, including:

✪ **Planning and organising**
✪ **Crowd management**
✪ **Stewarding**
✪ **Facilities for people with disabilities**
✪ **Communication**
✪ **Temporary structures**
✪ **Sound and noise**
✪ **Firefighting**
✪ **Traffic and transport arrangements**

Additional legislation

Many of the acts and regulations mentioned so far relate specifically to health and safety. There is, however, other legislation that needs to be taken into account when considering safety issues in the workplace. Pages 63 to 67 will look at four of them:

✪ **Disability Discrimination Act 1994**
✪ **Working Time Regulations 1998**
✪ **Data Protection Act 1998**
✪ **Children Act 1989**

Disability Discrimination Act 1994

This piece of legislation, introduced in 1995, was a major breakthrough for people with disabilities. Its main relevance to the leisure and recreation industry is in employment rights and service provision. From an employment viewpoint, it is unlawful for an employer to discriminate against a disabled person:

○ **In the arrangements in which it is determined who employment shall be offered to**

○ **In the terms on which offers of employment are made**

○ **By refusing to offer, or deliberately not offering, employment**

It is also unlawful to discriminate against a disabled person who is already involved in respect of such things as terms of employment, promotion, training, etc. From a service provision viewpoint, it is unlawful for a provider to discriminate against a disabled person:

○ **In refusing to provide, or deliberately not providing, any service offered (or prepared to be provided) to members of the public**

○ **In the standard of service provided**

The act has had a significant impact on the industry as Part III clearly states that the legislation applies to:

○ **Access to and use of any place which members of the public are permitted to enter (point 3a)**

○ **Facilities for entertainment, recreation or refreshment (point 3f)**

Activity 2.2

Investigate two contrasting leisure and recreation facilities to see how they comply with the act in respect of service provision. Feed back your findings to the group to see whether facilities are adhering to the legislation.

The act also established the National Disability Council to advise the Secretary of State on:

○ **Matters relevant to the elimination of discrimination against disabled persons**

- ✪ **On measures which are likely to reduce or eliminate such discrimination**
- ✪ **On matters related to the operation of the act**

The Countryside Commission

The Countryside Commission, an advisory body that promotes the countryside for open-air recreation and enjoyment, published a practical guide for countryside managers on recreation for people with disabilities. Its introduction sums up the barriers that exist for people with disabilities in accessing countryside recreation:

The freedom and refreshment of being out in the country is just as necessary and enjoyable to the minority of people who are permanently disabled as it is to able-bodied people – perhaps more so. Yet all too often the countryside experienced by people with disabilities is marred, not only by their disability or mobility aids, but by an environment that has been modified by able-bodied people for able-bodied people. It is not only people with disabilities that are excluded from enjoying the benefits of the countryside, the elderly, the young and even pregnant women all face similar problems.

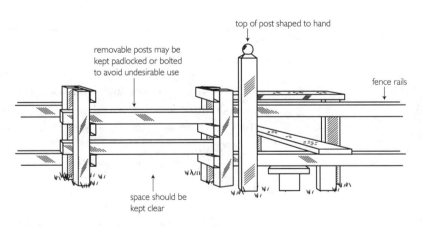

This stile improves accessibility

continued

continued

The guide gives excellent advice on such areas as:

★ Designing to increase accessibility in the countryside

    car parks

    paths

    handrails

★ Providing information

★ Informal recreation activities in the countryside

★ Transport

Working Time Regulations 1998

The Working Time Regulations came into effect on 1 October 1998 and covered the following areas:

- ✪ **Working time**
- ✪ **Rest periods**
- ✪ **Breaks**
- ✪ **Paid holiday entitlements**
- ✪ **Night workers**
- ✪ **Young workers**

The regulations were primarily concerned with protecting workers' rights on the amount of hours they were legally expected to work.

Data Protection Act 1998

The Data Protection Act requires all organisations that hold personal information about individuals on a manual, automated or computerised system to comply with the act. Organisations that hold more than standard information, e.g. accounts, need to register with the Office of the Data Protection Registrar. The 1998 Act strengthens and extends the 1984 Act which requires organisations to:

- ✪ **Obtain and process any information fairly and lawfully**
- ✪ **Only hold the information for its stated purpose**
- ✪ **Not disclose the information to anyone else unless previously stated**
- ✪ **Only hold information suitable and sufficient for the purpose**
- ✪ **Ensure the information is accurate and up to date**
- ✪ **Only hold the information for as long as is necessary**
- ✪ **Allow access, at reasonable intervals, to persons who have information held about them**
- ✪ **Make reasonable security measures to ensure against unauthorised access**

Many leisure and recreation organisations now rely very heavily on information technology, hence they fall within the bounds of the Data Protection Act. Information often stored on computerised systems includes:

- ✪ **Membership details**
- ✪ **Booking and reservation details**
- ✪ **Financial details**

Children Act 1989

The Children Act came into force in October 1989 and contained new regulations that affected everyone who had responsibility for planning, managing and delivering services to children. The main impact on the leisure and recreation industry was the need to ensure consistent standards of care and common frameworks for provision, which included powers to ensure staff working with children receive appropriate training opportunities.

The act contains a lot of information, much of which has little relevance to leisure providers. On the other hand, providers do need a good working knowledge in these three areas:

- ✪ **Coordinating and delivering children's playschemes, sports activities, adventure holidays, etc.**
- ✪ **Providing information to the public on services for which they are directly responsible**
- ✪ **As a body of expertise due to their major involvement in providing services for children outside of school, especially children under age 8**

Child protection is also important in sport. There has been considerable evidence of wrongdoing by coaches in a variety of sporting activities. The

National Coaching Foundation (NCF) provides a range of training and information to coaches and it runs workshops on good practice and child protection. It has taken a leading role in child protection issues in sport and developed resources to support this initiative. Two governing bodies of sport, the Badminton Association of England (BAoE) and the Rugby Football Union (RFU), have both recently united with the NCF to implement awareness and protection issues.

Codes of practice

Approved codes of practice

Codes of practice elaborate on the implementation of regulations contained in health and safety legislation and are prepared by the HSC after consultation with interested bodies. Not following a code of practice is not a breach of the regulation in itself, but if an act or regulation is contravened then failure to follow an approved code of practice (ACOP) would be seen as evidence that all reasonable steps were *not* taken to adhere to the regulation.

Voluntary codes of practice

Many organisations in the leisure and recreation industry prepare codes of practice to provide guidance to their members. In the UK the Royal Life Saving Society (RLSS) has a code of practice on training and assessing. It is used as a reference guide in all cases of uncertainty or dispute. It enables the RLSS to:

- **Establish common and consistent standards of training and assessing**
- **Develop agreed practices in all areas of lifesaving and lifeguarding**
- **Identify systems which are compatible with NVQs**
- **Maintain high levels of performance, support through moderation and quality assurance programmes**
- **Identify links with current RLSS policy statements and guidance notes**
- **Provide regular and effective in-service and update training**
- **Ensure that training and assessing records are processed and kept up to date**
- **Set up effective and disciplinary procedures**

Try to find examples of other voluntary codes of
practice from the leisure and recreation industry. They
may prove useful later on in your programme.

Hazards and risk assessment

Risk assessment

A varied and diverse industry such as leisure and recreation carries with it a
range of hazards and dangers. From a small dry-side leisure centre through to a
major international theme park, there is real potential for employees and
members of the public to injure or harm themselves.

The Management of Health and Safety at Work Regulations 1992 recognise
that many accidents could be prevented if their potential to cause harm had
been previously recognised and acted upon. For this reason they require every
employer to carry out a suitable assessment of:

✪ **The health and safety risks their employees are exposed to at
work**

✪ **The health and safety risks that arise out of their conduct
towards persons not in their employment**

This legislation is of particular relevance to an industry that employs large
numbers of people and relies on customer visits for the bulk of its business. To
comply with the regulations, employers must conduct what is known as a risk
assessment. Various approaches are possible, often dependent on the size,
scale and main business of an organisation. However, whatever the approach,
a risk assessment must:

✪ **Identify all hazards associated with the organisation**
✪ **Record the significant findings (if more than five people are
employed)**
✪ **Identify employees and/or members of the public who may be
at risk**
✪ **Evaluate existing controls to ascertain whether they are
suitable; if not, state the measures to be taken**

- Judge and record the likelihood of an accident occurring as a result of an uncontrolled risk

- Judge and record the severity if an accident were to occur as a result of an uncontrolled risk

- Prepare an action plan to prioritise the necessary measures for controlling identified risks

- Implement measures, including training and the dissemination of information

- Monitor and amend the implemented measures

Hazard
something that has the potential for harm

Risk
the likelihood of the harm occurring and the severity of its consequences

A person conducting a risk assessment must be 'suitably experienced' in the operation or activity so they can accurately identify the relevant **hazards** and **risks**. However, before the risk assessment can be undertaken, it is important to clarify key terminology.

Conducting a risk assessment

Before a risk assessment is carried out, it is good practice to list all the operations or activities undertaken within the organisation. Then nothing should be overlooked.

Hazard identification

Complex activities are usually broken down into simpler activities. A large ride at a theme park could be broken down into these operations:

- **Loading customers**
- **Unloading customers**
- **Normal operating procedure**
- **Emergency action plan**
- **Breakdown of equipment**
- **Cleaning of equipment**
- **Routine maintenance**
- **Installation procedures**
- **Dismantling procedures**

Typical hazards from loading customers could include:

- **Customers slipping while entering the ride**
- **A safety harness or restraint not working**
- **Too many customers on the ride**
- **Customers entering the ride at wrong locations**

A theme park ride has many operations
(Courtesy of Thorpe Park)

An experienced ride operator would be the ideal person to identify the possible hazards associated with loading customers.

Risk assessment

There are two factors to risk assessment: the likelihood of the harm occurring and the severity of the harm if it does occur. This scale could be used to obtain the likelihood factor:

5 = certain to occur
4 = very likely to occur
3 = likely to occur
2 = unlikely to occur
1 = very unlikely to occur

And this scale could be used to obtain the severity factor:

5 = death or fatal injury

4 = major injury (reportable under the Reporting of Injuries, Diseases and Dangerous Occurrences Regulations)

3 = lost time injury (not reportable under RIDDOR)

2 = minor injury

1 = delay only

Each hazard can then be given a risk ranking by multiplying the likelihood factor with the severity factor. Priorities are determined accordingly.

Once priorities have been decided, it is possible to think about the measures required to control the risk. The most obvious measure is to conduct the activity in a different, less risky manner. If this is not possible, try to reduce the likelihood of the harm occurring. Here is a good example from a swimming pool; it could be recorded using the documentation on page 72.

- ✪ **Activity: male changing rooms in the swimming pool access the pool area at the deep end**
- ✪ **Hazard: entering deep water**
- ✪ **Persons in danger:**

  non-swimmers

  young swimmers

- ✪ **Severity: drowning (death, grade 5)**
- ✪ **Likelihood: unlikely to occur (grade 2)**
- ✪ **Risk ranking: 10 (priority 2)**
- ✪ **Control measures required: the hazard cannot be removed unless expensive alterations are made to the changing room. Therefore the following measures could be implemented:**

  warning notices in changing rooms

  warning notices at deep end

  barriers erected at deep end (to restrict entry)

  lifeguard presence at deep end (at all times)

In all cases target dates for implementation should be set and specific actions given to named personnel. It is also good practice to record when control measures have been implemented. Information sheets, clarifying risks, control measures and detailing training needs can be used to enhance the risk assessment process.

Monitoring risk assessment

It is not sufficient to conduct a risk assessment and then consign the documentation to the filing cabinet. It needs to be monitored and reviewed at regular intervals then updated if control measures are found to be inadequate or new methods are implemented.

CLUB RISK ASSESSMENT FORM

Club: ....

Date of Assessment: ....

HAZARDS

While playing, what hazards could you reasonably expect to come across that are likely to cause you harm that would require medical attention?

e.g. *Slippery floors, Damaged wire netting, Contact with an opponent, Equipment*

....

....

WHO IS AT RISK?

What groups would be affected by the hazard?

e.g. *Players, Spectators, Beginners/Novices, Umpires/Coaches*

....

....

HAZARD CONTROL

At present what do you do to control the hazard?

e.g. *Adequate information, Safety checks on equipment, Full complement of qualified officials*

....

....

FURTHER ACTION

What could you do to reduce the risk of an accident?

e.g. *Check equipment – balls/posts, Get qualified officials*

....

....

FURTHER ACTION

The following changes are required to our Club's Code of Conduct:

....

....

I declare that the above information is true and accurate.

Signed: .... Date: ....

A new risk assessment form must be completed at the start of each season, to ensure you cover the club should the incident happen again and any resultant changes made to the club's code of conduct.

It is the responsibility of the club Chair/Secretary to ensure that equipment is regularly checked and repaired, and that members are informed of any risks.

How to set out a risk assessment

All England Netball Association

The All England Netball Association (AENA) takes the safety of its players, coaches and spectators very seriously. To ensure consistency throughout its many clubs and associations, the AENA has produced a booklet that covers a range of safety information and advice. It includes information on child protection and the following areas:

★ Duty of care and risk assessment

★ Child protection for all its members

★ AENA child protection procedures

★ Code of conduct for young players

★ Code of conduct for volunteers

The introduction to the guideline gives a good summary of AENA's stance on health and safety:

Children and young people are the future of netball. Every child who participates in netball should be able to do so in a fun, safe environment and be protected from harm. The AENA places the highest priority on their safety. The aim of this guide is to highlight the importance of our duty of care. The objectives are that by the end of this guide your club/association will:

★ Have a clear understanding of what duty of care is

★ Appreciate why the paperwork is necessary for your club/association

★ Be able to complete the necessary paperwork

It goes on to offer this definition for 'duty of care':

The duty which rests upon an individual or organisation to ensure that all reasonable steps are taken to ensure the safety of any person involved in

continued

continued

any activity for which that individual or organisation is responsible.

The guide continues to give excellent advice on all aspects of safety and provides readers with easy to complete proformas such as the club risk assessment form (page 72) and interview questions.

E © 1999 AENA

NETBALL INTERVIEW QUESTIONS FOR HELPERS WITH YOUNG PEOPLE

It is unlikely that you will be able formally to interview all the volunteers who want to help. Therefore use these questions as reminders of what you should be asking when new volunteers want to help with young people.

Name: _____

Date: _____ Time: _____

Use the boxes as a check (✓) to ensure you ask all the questions.

1. Tell us about yourself.	☐
2. What attracted you to apply to help at this club? What special skills can you bring to the club?	☐
3. Have you any previous experience of working with children?	☐
4. Tell us about a successful experience you have had working with children and why it worked well.	☐
5. Tell us about an unsuccessful experience you have had working with children and why. What would you do next time to put it right?	☐
6. Questions relating to the application form. (If applicable)	
•	☐
•	☐
7. What do you think makes a 'good' activity session in the opinion of the children?	☐
8. What makes a 'good' activity session in your view (bearing in mind the aim of the Club is to provide a quality learning experience in an enjoyable way)?	☐
9. HEALTH & SAFETY – It is important that the Club runs safely. Using your knowledge of the facilities, what steps would you recommend to make sure the Club is as safe as possible for the children?	☐

18 NSPCC CHILD PROTECTION HELPLINE 0800 800 500

Some questions AENA uses to interview its youth workers
(Courtesy of All England Netball Association)

Ensuring a safe working environment

All leisure and recreation facilities need to adopt procedures and good practice to ensure the safety of staff and customers at all times. If a systematic approach to health and safety is implemented, the likelihood of incidents occurring will be greatly reduced. It is also important that all employees support a safety-first culture and cooperate fully with directives and initiatives aimed at providing an enjoyable but safe environment.

Unfortunately, accidents will always happen, but measures can be taken to ensure they are minimised. In addition to risk assessment, the following procedures should be adopted by any organisation that takes health and safety seriously.

Staff training

Induction

A continual programme of staff training should be in place to ensure all employees have an understanding of what is required of them at work. All new members of staff need to undergo a comprehensive induction to the organisation, and health and safety should be an essential part. It needs to cover:

- **Employee responsibilities under health and safety legislation**
- **Emergency procedures (fire, first aid, suspicious packages, etc.)**
- **Dealing with accidents and report writing**
- **Hazard identification**
- **Safe handling of equipment and substances hazardous to health**

Heanor Leisure Centre

Heanor Leisure Centre is one of four leisure centres in the borough of Amber Valley. It is a busy multi-purpose facility with an annual throughput of approximately 220 000 visitors per year. The centre has an extensive induction

continued

continued

programme for all staff which covers general areas (a tour of the workplace, how to complete timesheets, etc.) and then items for specific jobs. Here is an example of some induction material for bar staff. A similar format is used to cover emergency procedures, accident or incident reporting and relevant legal knowledge.

HEANOR LEISURE CENTRE

STAFF INDUCTION CHECKLIST

BAR STAFF

THE FOLLOWING TOPICS SHOULD BE COVERED WITHIN THE FIRST THREE DAYS WHERE POSSIBLE

Trainer initials ....

Employee signature ....

Safety Issues

(a) Health and Safety at Work Act – explain briefly what the act entails and implications to the employee

(b) COSHH regulations – explain briefly what the regulations entail

(c) RIDDOR – explain briefly, giving guidelines of procedure, when to report and responsibilities of employer and employee

(d) Inspecting electrical equipment and flexes, power points, plugs, sockets PAT test dates, etc., before use

(e) Danger signs, out-of-order signs

(f) Handling electricity – dos and don'ts

(g) Lifting and carrying large and heavy items

(h) Use of ladders

(i) Use of fire extinguishers for small fires – identifying correct extinguishers

---

All organisations are required to prepare a written statement of their health and safety policy and ensure adequate arrangements are made to carry it out. It is essential therefore that new employees are issued with relevant literature so they can refer to it as and when required. Anyone starting a new job will find it extremely difficult to digest all the information directed at them, so a staff handbook can be very useful in those hectic first weeks.

Most organisations now have a document known as a normal operating procedure (NOP). This will explain how the facility operates on a day-to-day basis and is fundamental in the delivery of safe products and services. A typical leisure centre may include these items in its NOP for a swimming pool:

- **Pool dimensions and depths**
- **Water testing procedures and actions**
- **Acceptable water readings**
- **Poolside access and egress**
- **Bather loads**
- **Lifeguard/bather ratios**
- **Lifeguard duties and rosters**

Activity 2.4

Choose a leisure and recreation facility, perhaps a cinema or a nightclub, and note down what information *you* would expect to find in their normal operating procedures. You could check afterwards to see if you were right.

Emergency action plans (EAPs) explain staff procedures and actions during emergencies or an evacuation. Here are some of the eventualities they cover:

- **Fire**
- **Power failure**
- **Gas or chemical leak**
- **Structural damage**
- **Missing person**
- **Serious injury**
- **Bomb threat**

All facilities will have EAPs to suit their particular needs. Staff need to be aware of their content, and EAPs are often an integral part of training. Like all

FIRE SAFETY INSTRUCTIONS
for
NEW TOWN FOOTBALL CLUB

FIRE ALARM

The fire alarm system is:

A CONTINUOUS VOICE ANNOUNCEMENT OPERATED BY
BREAK GLASS CALL POINTS

IF YOU DISCOVER A FIRE:

1. **Operate the nearest fire alarm.**

2. **Immediately vacate the premises by the nearest available exit and proceed to the assembly point indicated below.**

DO NOT RE-ENTER THE BUILDING TO COLLECT PERSONAL BELONGINGS.

If it is SAFE to do so tackle the fire with the nearest appropriate fire extinguisher. Always ensure there is a safe exit route before attempting to extinguish any fire.

WHEN INFORMED OF A FIRE:

1. **Immediately vacate the premises by the nearest available exit.**

2. **Proceed to the assembly point indicated and await roll call.**

ASSEMBLY POINT:

CAR PARK

**DO NOT RE-ENTER THE BUILDING UNTIL TOLD TO DO SO BY
MANAGEMENT, UNDER INSTRUCTION BY THE SENIOR FIRE OFFICER**

Fire safety at a football club

procedures, their effectiveness needs to be monitored and they should be updated regularly.

Ongoing training

Leisure and recreation operates in an ever changing world, so it is important that staff undergo regular training to refresh their current practice or to learn new skills. Effective staff training requires a well-planned schedule, proper resourcing and adequate time off.

Regular inspections

Although staff should constantly be on the lookout for problems with equipment and the fabric of the building, regular checks need to be undertaken to ensure equipment is safe for use. It is important that *all* equipment is inspected, its condition logged and remedial action taken to rectify any faults.

A typical outdoor adventure organisation, specialising in canoeing, climbing, abseiling and hillwalking, has a wide range of operational and safety equipment. All of it needs inspecting on a regular basis to meet the rigorous licensing requirements.

Outdoor education equipment

- ✪ **Minibuses and other transport**
- ✪ **Trailers for canoes, etc.**
- ✪ **Canoes and kayaks**
- ✪ **Full canoe kit (paddles, buoyancy aids, helmets)**
- ✪ **Canoe safety and rescue kits**
- ✪ **Climbing harnesses, crabs, figure of eight, helmets**
- ✪ **Lead ropes, top ropes, abseil ropes**
- ✪ **Rucksacks**
- ✪ **Teaching and expedition compass**
- ✪ **First aid kits**
- ✪ **Gaiters, strobes, flares and Karrymore Instructors' Survival Kit (KISU)**
- ✪ **Survival bags**

Activity 2.5

Devise your own proforma to record the findings of an equipment inspection. It needs to contain these items:

- ★ Name of equipment
- ★ When checked
- ★ Name of person checking equipment
- ★ Results of check
- ★ Any action taken
- ★ Signature of inspector

If equipment is highly specialised or technical it may be necessary for experts to perform inspections. If this is the case a maintenance contract needs to be in place with a suitable organisation who can perform the necessary checks and repairs. Close monitoring is required to ensure conditions are being adhered to and standards maintained.

It is not only equipment that needs regular inspection. Faults with the structure of buildings (and associated areas) can contribute to serious safety hazards if not identified and rectified. Safety audits, similar to equipment checks, need to be conducted on a regular basis. The results need to be logged and action taken to correct any deficiencies or problems. The following areas may feature prominently on any safety audit:

✪ **Car park, footpaths, steps and approaches to facilities**

✪ **External lighting, fencing and security cameras**

✪ **External activity surfaces such as grass and tarmacadam**

✪ **Internal and external windows and means of access or egress**

✪ **Internal walkways, carpeted areas and spectator areas**

✪ **Damaged or dangerous tiles and other surfaces**

✪ **Storage areas**

Budgeting for health and safety

As health and safety is an integral part of leisure and recreation, it requires a commitment from management to allocate sufficient funds for training, equipment, maintenance and monitoring. As with other areas of operation, a separate budget needs to be allocated for health and safety. This will be reviewed and reassessed in line with the financial codes of practice within the organisation.

Activity 2.6

Contact a range of leisure and recreation providers in your area and ask how much finance they allocate to health and safety each year. If possible, break the figures down into categories such as:

★ Equipment

★ Training

★ Information

Seeking advice on health and safety

A range of organisations can help with advice and information on health and safety issues. The HSE, local authorities and fire authorities are usually very keen to impart safety advice. Other possible sources include:

- ✪ **Health and safety consultancies**
- ✪ **Governing bodies of sport**
- ✪ **National training boards**
- ✪ **Trade organisations**

Security in leisure and recreation

Statistics show that certain crimes are on the decrease, after years when the trend was always upwards. However, security is still a major concern for most people in this country and the leisure and recreation industry is no different in this respect.

Security of staff

One of the most worrying aspects in recent years is the upsurge in acts of violence towards staff working in the industry. Although the industry is not unique – it is commonplace to see nurses, teachers and firefighters the victims of assault – employers must give paramount importance to security if their staff are to feel secure when undertaking duties connected to their position. In any service occupation, where there is a high degree of contact between staff and the public, the potential for conflict is very real. This is heightened by the fact that many customers in the industry can quickly become overexuberant or demanding.

The most common types of incident involve verbal abuse which, although not as serious as a physical assault, can cause the recipient great distress. Any type of threat, whether verbal or physical, can cause anxiety among staff. This can lead to low morale, absenteeism, high staff turnover and the economic consequences they bring.

To counteract the ever rising incidents of verbal and physical attacks, many organisations now train their staff in such areas as managing angry customers and basic protection against assault techniques. Other organisations employ staff specifically to deal with unruly customers. Many pubs now have door supervisors who control entry to the premises and are quickly on hand to deal with any troublemakers. Pubs also operate exclusion schemes for people found guilty of offences on licensed premises.

Professional football clubs provide an excellent example of how the security of staff and customers can be enhanced through training and the use of technology. Most grounds now have sophisticated surveillance operations closely monitored within control stations at the ground. Coupled with the support from trained stewards, this has dramatically reduced the incidents of violence at football matches over recent years.

When incidents do occur they should be logged so that an organisation can monitor particular problem areas and act accordingly. The HSE recommends a seven-point plan to address abuse or violence in the workplace:

1 **Ask staff if there is a problem**
2 **Record all incidents**
3 **Classify incidents**
4 **Identify preventative measures**
5 **Identify the most relevant measures**
6 **Put the measures into practice**
7 **Monitor the measures and modify them if necessary**

The control room at a modern stadium
(Courtesy of Wembley National Stadium Ltd)

Activity 2.7

Visit a leisure organisation in your locality where you think staff and visitor security may be an issue. Find out what problems do exist and how the organisation addresses them.

Security of property

All leisure organisations are only too aware of the high cost of replacing damaged or stolen equipment. It is important therefore that measures are taken to ensure the security of building contents, money, the building itself and customer property.

Building contents

Many leisure organisations use expensive equipment and technology; this equipment can be vulnerable when the facility is open as well as when it's closed. Security is the responsibility of all employees. Vigilant staff can very often prevent thefts just by being aware of suspicious individuals and their movements. Here are some other methods:

- ✪ **Restricting entry to customers who have legitimate reasons to be on the premises**
- ✪ **Ensuring all equipment is security marked with the organisation's name**
- ✪ **Ensuring all equipment is stored in secure storage areas**
- ✪ **Installing security cameras in sensitive areas**
- ✪ **Regular stock checks to deter theft and misuse by employees**
- ✪ **Regular checks of vulnerable points of entry such as fire escapes**
- ✪ **Restricting access to areas where expensive equipment is used or stored**

Money

Most recreation facilities have lots of money on their premises. Money poses a security risk and must be safely deposited using appropriate systems and procedures. To reduce the risk of theft or misappropriation, facilities should:

- ☺ **Ensure the public have no access to areas where money is taken or handled**
- ☺ **Limit access to essential staff only**
- ☺ **Keep safe keys and combinations secret**
- ☺ **Install security cameras in areas where money is handled**
- ☺ **Install alarms where cash handling is undertaken**
- ☺ **Brief staff on the procedures for safe handling of cash**
- ☺ **Ensure sensitive areas are secure and remain locked at all times**
- ☺ **Train staff how to deal with security incidents involving money**

Preventing fraud

Gone are the days when customers purchased goods or services predominantly with cash. The alternatives may be more convenient but they can be used fraudulently. Here are three common ways:

- ☺ **Personal cheques**
- ☺ **Credit cards**
- ☺ **Debit cards**

Personal cheques

Many customers now pay for leisure and recreation services by cheque. When accepting a cheque, ensure it is has been completed correctly and is not being used fraudulently. There are four things to do:

Many customers pay by cheque

- ✪ Check the date is correct; never accept post-dated cheques
- ✪ Make sure the cheque is made payable to the correct organisation
- ✪ See that the amount in figures matches the amount in words
- ✪ Verify that the signature agrees with the name printed on the cheque

A valid cheque guarantee card should accompany all cheques. These can vary in value from £50 to £250. Look at the card to ensure:

- ✪ The expiry date has not passed
- ✪ The card details agree with the cheque details:
    - account name
    - sort code
    - account number
- ✪ The signature on the card matches the signature on the cheque

Many cheque guarantee cards now carry a picture of the cardholder. This makes validating ownership much easier and reduces the risk of stolen cards or cheques being used. If you are unsure about the validity of cheques or guarantee cards, ask for further proof of identification or consult your line manager. If any doubt persists, politely refuse the cheque.

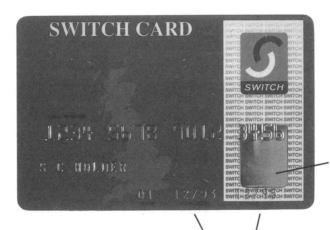

cheque guarantee limit hologram will appear here or on the back

check from and to dates

Ask for a valid guarantee card
(Courtesy of Switch Card Services Ltd)

Debit cards and credit cards

A debit card, such as Switch or Delta works in a similar way to a cheque. The amount of the transaction is debited from the holder's account electronically. A credit card such as MasterCard or Visa allows the cardholder instant credit, authorised in advance by the credit company.

Be vigilant when customers are purchasing with a debit or credit card. If the customer is present, the card needs to be swiped through the EFTPOS equipment (electronic funds transfer at point of sale); this will either allow or refuse the transaction.

One major advantage of debit cards and credit cards is that they can be used to purchase goods or services over the telephone. In the leisure and recreation industry they could be used to pay for theatre tickets, hotel accommodation or mail-order sportswear. Obtain the following information when accepting payment over the phone:

- **Card number**
- **Expiry date**
- **Issue number**
- **Name on the card**
- **Card billing address**

If you are suspicious about the card presented to you, call an authorisation centre to verify its validity. If the card is found to be stolen or suspicious, it should be retained and dealt with in accordance with the card organisation's procedures.

A successful transaction generates two receipts, one for the customer and one for the retailer. Check the customer's signature is okay on the signed receipt.

Debit cards are not the same as credit cards
(Courtesy of HSBC)

Buildings and fabric

Large leisure facilities can often be the target for mindless vandalism and damage. If the damage is not repaired, buildings can soon become unsightly and perhaps attract further vandalism. It is hard to eliminate all vandalism, but try to keep it as low as possible. Here are some steps you can take:

- **Use closed-circuit television (CCTV) to monitor vulnerable areas**
- **Employ security guards to patrol the exterior of buildings**
- **Install security lighting in high-risk areas**
- **Choose materials that are graffiti resistant or easy to clean**

Think how to keep your buildings secure from intruders. Again, a few simple steps will help:

- **Fit intruder alarms and have them monitored**
- **Ensure external doors are fitted with high-quality locks**
- **Have regular staff patrols to check on vulnerable access points**
- **Get advice from security experts**

Customer property

Protect the personal property of customers using your facilities. Business will soon suffer if visitors believe their property will be damaged or stolen. Here are some useful measures:

- **Advise customers to bring only essential items**
- **Tell customers to be vigilant**
- **Provide lockers for day-to-day items**
- **Provide security lockers for valuables**

Theft of information

Most organisations now rely heavily on computer systems, microfiche and videotape to record the information they need. The Data Protection Act ensures this information is not abused by organisations but it cannot guarantee security.

Compared with paper, storage media such as diskettes and CD-ROMs are much more vulnerable to accidental damage and deliberate theft. Treat computer files with the same level of security as you give to money. Make sure you set up the necessary passwords, protocols and firewalls. And here are some steps to prevent accidental damage:

- ✪ **Effective computer training for staff**
- ✪ **Helplines that give immediate help**
- ✪ **Backup copies stored in separate locations**
- ✪ **Safe storage in fireproof cabinets**

Revision questions

1   What are an employer's main responsibilities under the Health and Safety at Work etc. Act 1974?

2   What does COSHH stand for and what four main areas does it cover?

3   What gave rise to the Fire Safety and Safety at Sports Ground Act 1987?

4   Who enforces fire legislation?

5   What are the six health and safety directives introduced by the European Union in 1993?

6   How is health and safety enforced?

7   Briefly summarise the Working Time Regulations 1998.

8   List four types of licence a leisure and recreation facility may need.

9   What is the difference between a hazard and a risk?

10 Where might you seek advice on health and safety issues?

11 What act established the National Disability Council?

12 How can the security of money be maximised in a leisure facility?

13 When accepting a personal cheque what must you look for?

14 What is the difference between a debit card and a credit card?

15 How can vandalism and damage be reduced inside and outside leisure facilities?

The sports industry

3

Objectives

- **The history and development of sport**
- **The organisation and financing of sport**
- **Key issues in sport**
- **Working in the sports industry**

Sport today is big business. Millions of people participate in it, thousands are employed within it and huge amounts of money are generated by it. This unit charts the history of sport, from the medieval hunt to the modern sports of today. It looks at the administration and funding of sport, its role in society and many key issues that now affect it. It also examines the benefits of health and exercise to individuals and communities. The unit concludes with a look at employment issues within the sports industry.

The history and development of sport

What is sport?

If you ask five people for their definition of sport, you will probably get five different answers. It is easy to name a specific sport, but much harder to define what makes a sporting activity. Nevertheless, it is generally accepted that a sport should:

- ✪ **Involve some type of physical activity**
- ✪ **Require an element of skill**
- ✪ **Contain rules and regulations**
- ✪ **Be in some way competitive or provide a challenge**

Even when these points are considered, arguments can still rage as to the merits of certain sports. Two examples are darts and snooker (snooker may soon be an Olympic sport). Although they do require skill, they do provide a challenge and they do have rules, they can hardly be said to involve much physical activity.

What can be stated though, with an element of confidence, is that sport is something most people have experienced at some time during their lives. Love it or loathe it, sport plays a major part in society today.

Classifying sports

Did You Know?

The three families of sport are:
- ✪ Athletics
- ✪ Games
- ✪ Gymnastics

In order for sporting activities to be analysed, by coaches or performers, they have been classified into groups or categories. Within each category the sports have a clear resemblance to one another and are often called families of sport.

Athletics family

Athletic sports require a competitor to be able to jump higher; run, swim or cycle faster; throw further or lift more than their competition. Performance is measured in terms of time taken (swimming race), distance covered (long jump) or weight lifted (power lifting).

Success often depends on the competitor harmonising technique and power (high jump, javelin, etc.), facilitated by rules that do not allow opponents to interfere with the performance of fellow competitors.

Most people have experienced some sport
(Courtesy of Allsport)

Games family

Games activities require competitors to gain territorial domination over opponents: scoring more runs in cricket or winning more points in tennis. In a sport like boxing, domination is achieved by rendering an opponent defenceless against attack.

Swimming performance is measured by time
(Courtesy of Allsport)

The games family is divided into five subcategories:

- ✪ **Invasion**
- ✪ **Net and racket**
- ✪ **Striking**
- ✪ **Accuracy**
- ✪ **Combat**

Tennis players must score points to win games
(Courtesy of Allsport)

Gymnastics family

Gymnastic sports require competitors to perform a range of movements or sequences. Ice skating is an example. Competitors are judged by their ability to adhere to predetermined standards; in other words, they must aim for perfect repetition. Technically demanding, gymnastic success relies on the interpretation of performance by a judge or judges. As with athletic activity, competitors cannot interfere with each other's performance.

Analysing sports

There are several reasons for analysing sports. Whether for coaching or for personal interest, five levels of analysis can be applied:

- ✪ *Structural*: **An investigation into the very nature of the sport. Rules and regulations, scoring systems and pitch dimensions all fall within this level**

- ✪ *Strategic*: **The tactics or decision making used by competitors or teams to gain an advantage**

Figure skaters aim for perfect repetition
(Courtesy of Teunis Versluis Fotografie)

- ✪ *Technical*: **The technical requirements of the sport. A defensive header in football or a square cut in cricket are excellent examples. It also analyses skill – the performance of a technique under pressure**
- ✪ *Physical*: **The body type (somatotyping) or physical requirements essential for the sport. Flexibility and muscular make-up would also form part of the analysis**
- ✪ *Psychological*: **The mental strength required for success. Concentration levels, coping with pain and the ability to think quickly all need to be considered**

How sport has developed

The origins of sport can be traced back to medieval times, when simple activities were played at festivals linked to religion or agriculture. Even before then, the ancient Olympics in Greece (776 BC) had combined sporting activity and religious celebration. As time progressed, the opportunities to participate in play were limited as spare time was often at a premium. But simple games did develop and soon they were played on a more regular basis, much to the concern of the Church, as gambling (often associated with sport) was becoming more and more popular.

Even the origins of football can be traced back to Tudor times (late fifteenth century), when gangs of men participated in an unruly, violent and often destructive form of the highly structured and organised game we see today. This early version of the game was known as mob football.

Sport was beginning to flourish. That was until the Stuart period of the 1600s when the rise of Puritanism saw play (and sport) as potentially harmful. The general lawlessness that accompanied many activities was frowned upon by the government, and strict controls were placed on participation in the interests of social order. But it wasn't all bad news for sport. The Puritan influence moved it away from lawlessness and sport gradually became more acceptable.

During the 1700s sport developed without influence from the state. Cricket started to emerge and the aristocracy began to support major sports such as horse racing and prizefighting. It was also a time where participants had the potential to gain financial rewards as competitions were on the increase.

The early 1800s saw major changes in sport. Industrialisation caused people to move from the country into the new urban areas. Poor working and living conditions, coupled with long and boring hours, produced a demand for physical recreation away from work and home. The drift away from country-based sports had begun. During this period association football and rugby football became immensely popular. Football, in particular, attracted large crowds of mainly working-class spectators.

Major influences at this time were the public schools. Sport, initially discouraged due to its rowdy nature, was embraced and developed (especially rugby and football). Other sports such as hockey and rowing also owe their popularity and development to the public schools.

As sport began to flourish so did the potential for making money. Gambling had been an integral part of sport for many years but with participation levels and popularity reaching an all-time high, many sports associations were faced with the dilemma of amateurism versus professionalism. A professional was someone who was deemed to receive financial reward for participating, whereas an amateur participated purely for fun and enjoyment. Even today many of the problems facing sport derive from this issue. Professionalised in the late 1990s, rugby union is finding the transition from amateur status difficult.

Many other sports go from strength to strength. After a recent dip in popularity, mainly due to hooliganism, football has never been so popular, especially the Premiership. State-of-the-art-stadiums and an influx of foreign stars are a testament to its popularity. Golf, hockey and basketball are also very popular.

Bolton Wanderers have a state-of-the-art stadium
(Courtesy of Bolton Wanderers FC)

Activity 3.1

Up to now the unit has given a very general history of sport in the UK. For a more detailed insight, choose a sport that interests you and chart its development over the years. If you are working in a group, maybe investigate the sports individually then compare your findings. Each of you could choose a different sport to look at. Present your work as an annotated chart.

Sport and society

Sport, it is often said, reflects the society in which it is played. It can tell us much about the history and culture of a nation and give an insight into the characteristics of the population that play it. Take American football, a technically advanced sport offering many underprivileged people the opportunity of stardom or social mobility. Its annual showcase, the Super Bowl, is unashamedly commercial. Compare this with American society which, like the sport, is highly technical, highly commercialised and driven by a desire to succeed. One reflects the other.

Sport can therefore be said to play a major role in many of today's societies. An excellent example is education. Schools, especially post World War II, recognised the importance sport could play in the development of individuals.

The Super Bowl is unashamedly commercial
(Courtesy of Allsport)

Lifelong physical activity coupled with a positive and competitive attitude helped prepare pupils for adulthood and its responsibilities.

The sale of school playing fields at the end of the twentieth century, local management of schools, a reduction in teachers' goodwill towards after-school sport and a drift away from competitive sport during the 1980s, have all contributed to a reduction in sporting opportunities at school. This is often blamed for a general drop in the current fitness levels of many young people as the habits adopted in their formative years often remain with them in adulthood.

The current situation in primary education exemplifies this problem. A focus on mathematics, English, science and information technology leaves many schools with little time to dedicate to sport and fitness. Many people associated with sport hope that the educational review in 2000 may once again identify sport as an integral part of a child's education and development.

Activity
3.2

Research the current situation with regard to sporting opportunity (in educational establishments) for the following age groups. During your research investigate any changes in provision over the past 20–30 years. The results should be quite interesting.

★ 5–7 years
★ 7–11 years
★ 11–16 years
★ 16+ years

On a more positive note, there are now much better opportunities for sports participation (or physical activity). Better health education, focusing on the benefits of exercise (Sports Council) and healthy eating (National Heart Foundation) have made people more conscious of the need to participate in physical activity and to generally adopt a more healthy lifestyle. An increase in both public and private sector sporting provision has helped to accommodate the population's desire for sports participation. Other issues connected to sport and society are covered on page 115.

The benefits of sport

Playing sport has always been a great way to improve a person's health and fitness, except for the risk of injury that accompanies any physical activity. The benefits of a healthy body include:

- ✪ **Improved ability to live everyday life**
- ✪ **Less chance of illness and ill-health in later life**
- ✪ **The chance to remain active for as long as possible**
- ✪ **Improving the quality of life**

Apart from these benefits, sport can also be a vehicle for personal development. Many of the skills or qualities developed through sports participation can lead to success in later life. Here are some examples:

- ✪ *Social interaction*: **Playing sport is an excellent way to develop communication, teamwork and leadership qualities. Team games in particular require a high level of cooperation and a respect for others, either teammates or opponents**
- ✪ *Self-discipline*: **Whether it be controlling aggression on the field of play, developing a sense of responsibility to others or just completing an arduous training regime, sport can enhance self-discipline**
- ✪ *Self-esteem*: **Many sports performers find their self-esteem is improved through participating or being successful in sport. The desire to be successful and the motivation this can produce are often replicated in their life away from sport**
- ✪ *Social mobility*: **Sport provides an opportunity for the socially disadvantaged to progress in life. There are many examples of people who have gone from rags to riches as a result of their sporting success. Frank Bruno openly admits that his involvement in boxing saved him from a life of crime and almost certain poverty**

Exercise 3.1

Frank Bruno is someone who has benefited from sport. Can you think of others who have benefited in similar ways? You can include:

- ★ Careers in sport (coach, teacher, etc.)
- ★ Educational scholarships to university
- ★ Careers in the media (presenter, journalist, etc.)

Frank Bruno made a good living out of boxing
(Courtesy of Allsport)

The organisation and funding of sport

Provision for sport can range from a small-scale swimming gala (organised by a local swimming club) through to international events such as the Olympic Games and the Football World Cup. However, without managerial, administrative and financial support many sports would simply not survive.

International organisations

The International Olympic Committee

Probably the most famous of all international sports organisations is the International Olympic Committee (IOC), the supreme authority of the Olympic movement. With headquarters in Lausanne, Switzerland, the IOC coordinates the actions of the international sports federations (ISFs) and national Olympic committees (NOCs); their responsibilities are considered on page 102. Very rich and very powerful, the IOC has many aims. Here are some of them:

- ✪ **To encourage the coordination, organisation and development of sport and sports competitions**
- ✪ **To ensure the regular celebrations of the Olympic Games**
- ✪ **To support and encourage the promotion of sports ethics**
- ✪ **To lead the fight against doping in sport**
- ✪ **To oppose any political or commercial abuse of sports and athletes**

Structure

The IOC's affairs are managed by an executive board and president (elected by secret ballot for an initial eight-year term). Any proposals made by the executive board must be approved by the general assembly of members, otherwise known as the IOC session. A team of administrative directors lead departments such as:

- ✪ **Finance**
- ✪ **Marketing**
- ✪ **Press services**
- ✪ **Public relations**
- ✪ **Legal affairs**

The legal affairs department has been very busy dealing with the corruption allegations connected to recent successful bids by Salt Lake City (Winter Games 2000) and Sydney (Summer Games 2000).

Funding

Private funding is the only source of financial support received by the IOC. The sale of television rights and marketing programmes are the main contributors. The funds received are shared out as follows:

IOC officials get pride of place at opening ceremonies
(Courtesy of Allsport)

- ✪ **49% for the organising committees of the Olympic Games**
- ✪ **51% divided into thirds between the federations, the Olympic committees and the IOC**

Sponsorship has also become a major source of income for the Olympic movement. Many multinational corporations pay for exclusive rights to market their products through the Olympics.

Activity 3.3

The television rights to broadcast the Atlanta games in 1996 cost the American television company NBC $456 million. Find out how much the television rights have cost the successful company for the Sydney games in 2000.

Exercise 3.2

Try to recall some of the major companies that sponsored the 1996 Atlanta games.

International sports federations

International sports federations (ISFs) are responsible for the overall international development, administration and organisation of their sport. Their main responsibilities are:

✪ **To formulate the rules of the sport**
✪ **To arrange sponsorship and television rights**
✪ **To organise events**

There are many ISFs and their headquarters are based all over the world. Here are some of the most well known:

✪ **International Amateur Athletics Association (IAAA)**
✪ **International Rugby Football Board (IRFB)**
✪ **Fédération Internationale de Basketball (FIBA)**

Fédération Internationale de Football Association (FIFA)

FIFA, the international sport federation for soccer, was founded in Paris on 21 May 1904. The foundation act was signed by authorised representatives from seven European associations, including France, Belgium, Spain and Sweden. Conspicuous by its absence was the English Football Association (founded in 1863); it decided not to participate in an international federation.

The first FIFA congress elected the Frenchman Robert Guerin as president. It was at this time that the first FIFA statutes were laid down. They included:

★ The exclusive right of FIFA to organise international competition

★ The forbidding of clubs and players to play simultaneously for different national associations

FIFA's first major success was to convince the English association to join. This was achieved in April 1905. The associations of Germany, Austria, Italy and Hungary (plus all the home nations) soon followed suit. Plans for

continued

continued

international competitions were discussed at this time. The English FA took initial responsibility and a tournament was held within the 1908 Olympic Games in London. England won.

Up until 1909 only European associations were involved in FIFA, which had adopted French as its official language. Between 1909 and 1913 the organisation expanded to include South Africa, Chile, Argentina and the USA to give a true international feel to the organisation.

The start of World War I in 1914 hampered the development of FIFA, and only the sterling efforts of the Dutch representative, Carl Hirschmann, kept the organisation alive. At the end of the war in 1919 he convened a meeting in Brussels on the initiative of the French president, Jules Rimet, who was later elected as chairman in 1921. Rimet presided for 33 years and during this time:

★ Membership rose to 85 associations

★ The first FIFA-administered World Cup took place in Uruguay in 1930; Uruguay won

★ The British associations returned after the traumas of two world wars

★ The World Cup trophy was named after him

The first two English presidents were Arthur Drewry (1955–61) and the more well-known Sir Stanley Rous (1961–74). During Rous's presidency England won the World Cup for the first time in 1966. The World Cup of 1966 was the first to be televised worldwide. Besides helping football expand, television rights also provide FIFA with much needed revenue. Up to 1966 it had come solely from profits of the World Cup competition.

When the Brazilian Joao Havelange was elected president of FIFA in 1974, he transformed a somewhat reserved federation into the dynamic and businesslike organisation we have today. With 197 member associations and over 200 million active members, FIFA may be the most popular sports federation in the world.

Activity 3.4

The FIFA case study provides a concise overview of how the organisation has developed. Your task is to choose an international sports federation and conduct a similar exercise. If you are working within a group, try to produce histories for several ISFs. Try to find out as much as possible about how each ISF is funded. Present your findings as an annotated chart.

UK organisations

Central government

The UK government has always tended to be more permissive than mandatory over sports legislation – it allows for provision rather than enforcing provision. Have a look at the diagram below. It shows how sports administration is currently organised in the UK.

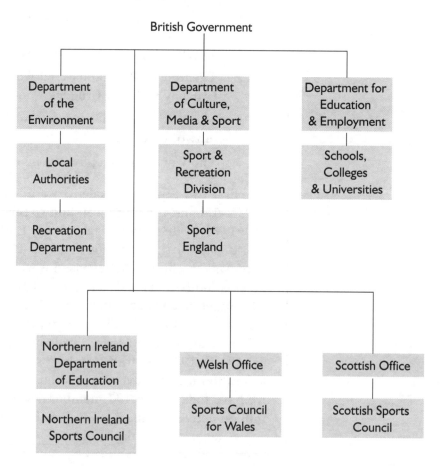

Many bodies look after sport in the United Kingdom

UK Sport and Sport England

▶ **HISTORY**

The UK government has never involved itself *directly* with the development of sport in the UK. That role falls to the national governing bodies of sport, all of them members of the British Sports Trust (formerly the Central Council for Physical Recreation). However, Dennis Howell, the minister for sport in 1966, established an advisory Sports Council to help the government on sporting matters. This was taken a stage further in 1972 when an independent Sports Council was established, by Royal Charter, with overall responsibility for sport in the UK. This organisation was given an annual grant by the government to help develop British sport.

▶ **CURRENT STRUCTURE**

In 1995 the then Department of National Heritage published 'Sport: raising the game', a policy paper which set out reorganisation plans for the current Sports Council. It was proposed to replace the existing Sports Council with a more streamlined structure consisting of two new bodies: the UK Sports Council and the English Sports Council. The Scottish, Welsh and Northern Ireland Councils were to remain.

The UK Sports Council and the English Sports Council came into existence towards the end of 1996. Now called UK Sport and Sport England, they are non-departmental organisations, they receive funding from the Department of Culture, Media and Sport (which replaced the Department of National Heritage) and they are accountable to that same department.

Did You Know?

Organisations such as the new sports councils are often known as Quangos:

QUA quasi
N non
G governmental
O organisation

Quangos are not under the direct control of government, but they are linked to government mainly through funding or policy accountability

UK Sport

UK Sport acts mainly as a coordinating body for the councils of England, Scotland, Northern Ireland and Wales. It currently receives an annual grant of £11.6 million from the Department of Culture, Media and Sport. Here are some of its interests:

- Attracting major sports events to the UK
- Marketing UK sports expertise abroad
- Performance and excellence in UK sport
- Doping control

Sport England

Sport England has three main policy areas:

- *Development of excellence*: **Development of excellence in sport through support of governing bodies and national sports centres**
- *Young people*: **To support youth sport in schools and to support other sports bodies such as the Youth Sports Trust by targeting resources and developing partnerships**
- *National Lottery*: **Distribution of grants from the Lottery Sports Fund**

Within these three policy areas it promotes women and sport, and sport for people with disabilities. Through extensive links with local authorities, governing bodies and commercial organisations, Sport England tries to develop the many facets of sport in England.

Sport England's ten regional offices coordinate policy making and provide information services, administrative support and sports science support. During the financial year 1998/99 it received a grant of over £33 million from the government. In addition, it distributed approximately £300 million as distributor of the Lottery Sports Fund in England.

Activity 3.5

Contact your regional council or your national council and request additional information on their work. Maybe arrange a visit where you can ask questions or discuss a topic in more detail.

National Lottery

The National Lottery has provided a major boost for UK sport since its introduction on 14 November 1994. Established to raise money for a variety of good causes, sport has benefited by well over £1 billion since the Lottery began.

Initially, only capital grants for the improvement or construction of facilities were available. However, from March 1997, there have been Lottery funds for individuals (in the form of revenue grants). This has benefited a whole range of top-quality performers, who can now spend more time training.

The first signs of success, directly linked to revenue grants, were the great results for British swimmers in the recent European Short Course Swimming Championships at Ponds Forge, Sheffield. A host of titles were won and new world records were set by James Hickman and Mark Foster. Their success was mainly attributed to financial support from Lottery grants.

Activity 3.6

Outstanding sports performers also receive grants from an organisation called the Sport Aid Foundation. Research the work of the foundation; find out:

★ When they were established

★ Their aims and objectives

★ How they are financed

★ How much grant aid they have commissioned

★ Which performers have benefited from their work

Governing bodies

Sports governing bodies have a range of functions. Besides representing the interests of their sport, they also:

- ✪ **Implement rules and regulations from their ISF**
- ✪ **Select national representative teams**
- ✪ **Organise competitions**
- ✪ **Develop coaching schemes and achievement awards**

The size of governing bodies varies. Some are very large, like the Rugby Football Union. Others are not so large, such as the British Water Ski Federation. What they do have in common is the desire to see their sport well supported and administered.

Governing bodies finance their operations in a variety of ways. Many receive grant aid from Sport England, with whom they have close contact. The Running Sport programme offers a range of support services to selected sports, including enhanced facilities and coaching excellence. Finance is also sourced from the many associations and clubs which affiliate to the governing bodies each year.

Channel 4 has bought television rights to some England Test matches
(Courtesy of Channel Four Television)

Sponsorship deals and television rights are increasingly important as sources of income. The decision by the Test and County Cricket Board (TCCB) to end their television deal with the BBC (and switch to Channel 4) will substantially increase their income in the next few years. Here are some major sponsorship deals negotiated by sports governing bodies:

- ✪ **Carling has sponsored Premiership football**
- ✪ **AXA has sponsored Sunday cricket**
- ✪ **BUPA has sponsored athletics events**

Exercise 3.3

See how many sponsorship deals you can recall from the past few years. Is there any special reason why you remember them?

National centres

Sport England is responsible for the five national sports centres which play a major part in the development of sports excellence in England. In conjunction with the sports governing bodies, Sport England provides excellent facilities, coaching and education at the following centres.

Bisham Abbey

Situated to the north-west of London, Bisham Abbey caters predominantly for weightlifting, tennis, squash, hockey and golf.

Holme Pierrepont

One of the premier watersports centres in the world, Holme Pierrepont provides excellence in canoeing, waterskiing and rowing. The British Canoe Union (BCU) has its base at this Nottingham centre.

Crystal Palace

Crystal Palace in south London boasts excellent indoor facilities. Its main sports include diving and athletics.

Plas y Brenin

Based in the Snowdonia National Park, Plas y Brenin is the national centre for mountain activities (including climbing and abseiling). Recent initiatives include management training programmes.

Lilleshall Hall

Football and gymnastics are the major sports at Lilleshall Hall, Shropshire. In addition, it houses an injury rehabilitation clinic specialising in sports medicine and physiotherapy.

Manchester Velodrome

A recent addition to the national sports centres is Manchester Velodrome. Cycling in the UK now has a focal point with excellent training facilities, coaching expertise and an arena to be proud of.

British Academy for Sport

The British Academy for Sport was the brainchild of the Conservative government. First mooted in the 1995 policy statement 'Raising the game', it was to be a £100 million state-of-the-art base for the sporting elite of the UK. The poor showing of Britain's Olympic team at the Atlanta games in 1996 (when only 15 medals were won) stiffened people's resolve to provide the best facilities and medical support in the world. After much deliberation a site in Sheffield was chosen as the home of the new institute. The renowned Australian Sports Academy (in Canberra) was to provide the blueprint for the British version and it was

continued

continued

hoped that the site at Don Valley would provide the impetus for success at the Sydney Olympics in 2000.

Unfortunately, the vision has yet to be realised. The project was beset by changes in direction and many major Olympic sports were reluctant to make it their home. Without a brick being laid, it is estimated that well over £750 000 (of Lottery money) has been spent on a series of meetings and discussions about 'the way forward'. It appears that much of the project is in limbo, with the original plans in doubt. A scaled-down version is much more likely, with support from the ten regional centres, and it is envisaged that sports such as cycling (Manchester), gymnastics (Lilleshall) and weightlifting (Bisham Abbey) will stay at their traditional bases. Only a few sports have given a commitment to use the Sheffield facility, and sports such as table tennis are intending to relocate there.

Activity 3.7

Research the major influences and players in the National Coaching Foundation (NCF) and the British Sports Trust (formerly CCPR).

Local and regional organisations

Sports organisations at regional and local levels support a range of activities and participants. The majority of sporting opportunities are provided by:

- **Local government**
- **Private clubs**
- **Education**
- **Commercial organisations**
- **Local sports clubs**

Local government

Although they have no legal obligation, local authorities still provide a whole range of sports facilities. The leisure and recreation department within local authorities will have a responsibility to provide facilities such as swimming pools, sports centres and parks. It is estimated that approximately 70% of all sports participation takes place at publicly funded facilities, with over 40% of this at the 1500 leisure centres within the UK.

Local authorities, like many organisations, work under tight financial control. Reductions in grants from central government, plus compulsory competitive tendering, have forced the public sector to adopt a more businesslike approach. Sports development officers (SDOs) have been appointed to encourage sports participation among a range of different groups; they have had a major impact in many areas.

Sports Development in Erewash Borough Council

Erewash Borough Council (EBC) in south-east Derbyshire has a population of over 106 000. The sports development officer for the authority has been in position since March 1998. The position is a joint venture between EBC and East Midlands Sports Council (EMSC); they fund the position on the following basis:

Year 1 100% EMSC 0% EBC

Year 2 50% EMSC 50% EBC

Year 3 0% EMSC 100% EBC

EBC's sports development strategy focuses on priorities such as:

★ Increasing the opportunities for participation and improved performance among people aged 4–18 throughout Erewash

★ Developing new partnerships and improving existing partnerships with agencies such as EMSC and sports governing bodies

continued

continued

Erewash council underlines its commitment to sport
(Courtesy Erewash Borough Council)

EBC's sports development unit has embarked on an extensive coach education programme in conjunction with the Derbyshire Sports Development Officer Forum, a partnership between the local authorities in the county. Their highly successful sports training and education programme (STEP) aims to improve the number and quality of sports coaches, officials and administrators throughout Derbyshire.

Education

Most schools, especially secondary schools, throughout England and Wales have extensive sports facilities. Many have entered into 'dual use' or 'joint provision' ventures with district councils to share facilities and make them available to the public outside of curriculum time. Many further and higher education facilities also encourage public use of their sports provision, as do private schools and colleges.

Private clubs

Private clubs attract members interested in the sport they provide. Predominantly funded through subscriptions and fees, some private clubs are very selective in their membership.

Activity 3.8

Locate a private sports club in your locality and find out:

★ How it is structured

★ How many members it has

★ The facilities and services it offers

Share your findings with classmates or colleagues.

Local clubs

Without the provision of local sports clubs, many people would be denied the opportunity to participate in organised sport. Whether the clubs play competitively or just for fun, they provide a valuable medium for enthusiasts to enjoy their particular sport.

A typical local sports club would fall within the voluntary sector, so it would rely on the goodwill of its members. Clubs can vary in size from a large swimming club, competing at regional or national level, to a small squash club only interested in local competitions. But both are likely to be affiliated to their respective regional association and national governing body.

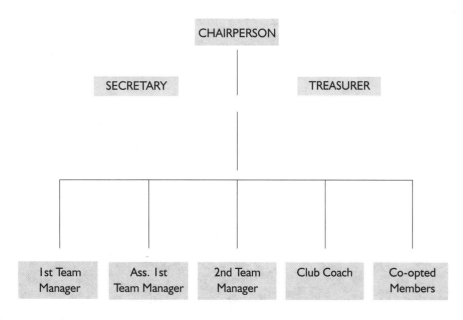

A local sports club could have this framework

The structure of a local sports club could look like the framework on page 113. A club of this size would rely heavily on the subscriptions paid by its members. It may also receive funding from these sources:

- ✪ **Social events and fund-raising activities**
- ✪ **Sale of sportswear, etc.**
- ✪ **Bar and catering receipts (if provided)**
- ✪ **Grants from a sports council or local authority**
- ✪ **Lottery grants**
- ✪ **Sponsorship deals with local business**
- ✪ **Donations**

Activity 3.9

Choose a sports club from your locality (you may be a member of it yourself) and find out about its structure and organisation. Try to obtain a copy of its financial incomings and outgoings. You may be surprised just how much it costs to keep a small club funtioning.

The private sector has quickly realised the appeal of sport and now provides a comprehensive range of sports facilities and opportunities throughout the UK. In order to survive, commercial organisations must make a profit. They identify gaps in provision and then cater for them. Often the gaps are facilities not provided by the public or voluntary sectors, e.g. health clubs, golf clubs and fitness centres (although some of these examples are provided by other sectors). Private sector facilities tend to be more exclusive and more expensive. In return the members expect excellent provision and high-quality products and services.

An excellent example from the private sector is David Lloyd Leisure Clubs. With state-of-the-art provision for indoor and outdoor tennis, squash, badminton and swimming plus well-equipped gymnasiums, the clubs can now be found in most major cities in the UK. Excellent sports provision combined with superb social facilities, that's David Lloyd's recipe for success.

Activity 3.10

Choose a sport you play or have an interest in and research its organisation from grass-roots level through to the international stage. Try to collate as much information as possible to help with your assessment.

Key issues in sport

Although sport can delight its many participants and spectators, it is seldom far from controversy. Sport often mirrors society, reflecting the negative aspects as well as the positive. Many people argue that without these negative aspects, sport would not hold such fascination for us; and perhaps by its very nature (physical, competitive, etc.) it will always have the potential for controversy. This section examines several related issues:

- **Political interference at the Olympic Games**
- **Drug taking within all sports**
- **Crowd violence at football matches**
- **Racism at football matches**
- **Violence on the rugby field**

Deviance in sport

Deviance is where individuals or groups break away from society's norms, often criminal behaviour. Deviance in sport occurs when participants break the rules, either written or unwritten. With the stakes so high, in many sports it is seen as inevitable that cheating will take place. Examples are well documented where competitors have tried to gain an advantage by cheating. Probably the most high-profile example in recent years is the Canadian sprinter Ben Johnson, who was stripped of his Olympic gold medal for drug taking; he was later banned from competition.

Exercise 3.4

Make a list of three different ways in which people cheat in sport and note down a few ideas as to why they use unfair methods to gain an advantage. Maybe organise a class debate on cheating in sport; it could be very revealing.

Drugs in sport

Although the use of drugs in competition can be traced back to the origins of sport itself, it is only recently (since the 1960s) that drugs have become a major concern. Advances in medicine have allowed many sportspeople to enhance their performance using chemical substances instead of training, diet and dedication.

The huge rewards for success are often cited as the reason why many people are prepared to risk the possible side effects of performance-enhancing drugs. They also risk being excluded from competition and being ostracised by fellow competitors if found guilty. For these people, the advantages appear to outweigh the disadvantages. Among other things, drugs can be used to:

✪ **Increase recovery rate after training**

✪ **Increase mental alertness**

✪ **Relieve pain**

✪ **Promote muscle growth**

The phenomenal success of former Eastern bloc countries such as the Soviet Union and East Germany has been attributed to state-sponsored drug abuse. Although drugs were not the only reason for success, they certainly contributed. Success for these athletes was seen as a victory for the political system they represented, vitally important during a tense period in global relationships.

It is not only the East that has experienced drug-related problems. Probably the most famous example from the West was the sprinter Ben Johnson as previously mentioned, although many other athletes have fallen foul of the administrators.

Not all drug use is linked to improving performance. Recent examples, especially from football, have featured so-called recreational drugs. Paul Merson, who has played for Arsenal and Middlesborough, confessed to having been addicted to drugs, alcohol and gambling. Paul Gascoigne, another Middlesborough player, has experienced problems with alcohol and has received help from the club and the Players Union.

Activity 3.11

The IOC, in conjunction with many national sports organisations, has an extensive programme of drug testing. Find out what these programmes are and use them as a basis for discussing the drugs issue with the rest of your group.

Violence in sport

Many sports have been beset with problems of violence, whether on the field or off. Violence on the pitch is often a result of frustration or a desire to win at all costs. An element of aggression is to be expected in many physical contact sports such as rugby and football, but many examples of players overstepping the mark have blighted their sport over the years.

Who can forget Eric Cantona and his 'fight' with a fan at Crystal Palace in 1995 or the mêlées at Five Nations rugby matches. Thankfully, these examples are still relatively rare, although they are still treated seriously by the clubs and sports governing bodies, who often fine and suspend the guilty parties.

Activity 3.12

Find out the disciplinary code for a sport of your choice. The county or regional association should have details of fines and sanctions available to them.

A far more worrying problem is spectator behaviour. There were terrible scenes at the Heysel stadium in Belgium before the European Cup Final between Liverpool and Juventus. Hooliganism, or the English disease, was a millstone around football's neck during the 1970s and 1980s. Weekly reports of pitch invasions, criminal damage and serious assaults often used to overshadow the matches themselves.

The turning point was the Hillsborough tragedy in 1989, when 96 supporters lost their lives. Lord Justice Taylor, in his report, attributed some of the blame to the perimeter fences erected to keep unruly spectators off the pitch. After the Taylor Report, fences were removed and the standing terraces were replaced by all-seater stadiums.

Other improvements in the game have helped reduce the problem of hooliganism, although the disruption caused by many England supporters at the 1998 World Cup in France show that the problem has not yet gone away completely. Safety improvement at football grounds include:

- ✪ **All-seater stadiums**
- ✪ **CCTV for police surveillance**
- ✪ **Improved training and vetting of stewards**
- ✪ **Improved facilities, including the removal of wooden stands**
- ✪ **Improved health, safety and security management**

Just when football seems to have eradicated many of its spectator problems, other sports are beginning to experience similar issues. Boxing, by its very nature, has always been controversial but it has never been associated with spectator violence. This all changed at the world title fight between Britain's Alan Minter and America's Marvin Hagler in the early 1980s when the crowd, disappointed at the Briton losing his crown, bombarded the ring with bottles and anything else they could throw. Hagler later described it as 'the most frightening experience of my life'.

This experience was the forerunner of frequent disturbances at many boxing events. Promoters at major events now employ security staff to control unruly spectators, but the recent death of a fan at a British title fight in Oldham was a tragic reminder that problems still exist.

Racism in sport

Like drug abuse and violence, racism is a major issue in sport today. Racism in sport reflects racism in society, and attempts to eradicate it have been at the forefront of many associations over the past few years. One of the most concerted efforts has been by the Professional Footballers Association (PFA) who, in conjunction with the Commission for Racial Equality (CRE), launched the campaign Let's Kick Racism out of Football.

Let's Kick Racism out of Football

The campaign was launched in response to a series of problems affecting the national game in this country. Abuse of Black players and the intimidation of ethnic minority supporters were rife at many grounds throughout the country.

In the 1993/94 season a series of high-profile launches and media events began to get the message across that racism was no longer acceptable in football. Well-known Black footballers such as Ian Wright and John Barnes threw their support behind the campaign and gave it added credibility.

In 1997 an independent organisation called Kick It Out was established. With funding from the PFA, the Football Association, the Football Trust and the Premier League, Kick It Out began its fight against racism. Here are some of its current projects:

continued

continued

★ Ensuring the campaign remains high profile at professional clubs throughout the Football League (and at conference level)

★ Working with grass-roots football to raise awareness at this level

★ To develop educational resources for young people in schools and colleges

★ To promote football participation with ethnic minority groups

Central to much of the organisation's work is partnership with other bodies at all levels of the game. Community groups, local authorities and police groups are just some examples of organisations working towards the good of the game.

Although racism is recognised as a problem in football, other sports have had their share of criticism over the years. High-profile sports such as tennis and golf are often criticised for their lack of top-level Black performers. Even in cricket, where there is high participation by non-whites, clubs such as Yorkshire have been put under the spotlight for not having any Black or Asian players in their team, despite the high numbers of Blacks and Asians living within the county.

Other sports seem to have had more success with integrating racial groups into their fold. Athletics and boxing have many top performers. Champions such as Linford Christie and Tessa Sanderson have achieved success at the highest level. This type of success has the effect of creating role models for future generations, and the next crop of exciting Black athletes is already emerging.

Even where racial groups are well established in a sport, there is still one area where ethnic minorities are poorly represented – management and administration. How many Black managers can you think of in football or boxing? How many ethnic minorities are represented in the administration of athletics?

Linford Christie and Tessa Sanderson: two champions
(Courtesy Allsport)

Exercise 3.5

Organisations such as the Rugby Football Union and the Lawn Tennis Association are developing inner-city programmes to broaden participation in their sports, often seen as middle class. What effect do you think this will have on ethnic minority participation and can you suggest any other ways to improve accessibility to groups often neglected in the past?

Sexism in sport

Statistics reveal that over 30% of males in the UK participate in sporting activity but only 10% of females. The population of the UK is almost equally split between males and females, so there appears to be a problem with female participation.

Many of the problems relate to past inequalities between men and women. It was only during the twentieth century that women won the right to vote and only during the past 30 years that governments began to address equal pay.

Today more and more women are challenging the stereotypes and outdated views that exist in many male-dominated activities. An excellent example is Wendy Toms. The first lineswoman in the Football League, she ran the line during a match between Torquay and Carlisle United in August 1994.

Less high profile, but just as significant, was the stance made by a 13 year old cricket-loving schoolgirl from Scotland. When Vari Maxwell was refused a trial by her district team – for being a girl – she embarked on a campaign with the Scottish Cricket Union aimed at proving girls were just as good at cricket as boys of a comparable age. So successful was Vari's campaign, the Scottish Union have since initiated extensive cricket development plans throughout the country.

As barriers to female participation in sport have been broken down, many previously held taboos have also been overcome. Although not accepted by everyone, women regularly play competitive football, cricket, rugby and even boxing. In fact, many of the national sides enjoy far more international success than their male counterparts.

Activity 3.13

Women are increasingly participating in more physically demanding sports such as rugby and boxing. Arrange for a debate in your class to argue points for and against such participation. Is there a general consensus or is opinion divided?

Politics in sport

Although the administration of sport strives fiercely to remain free from political influence, history suggests this has not always been possible. Many people argue that independence is impossible when organisations such as UK Sport rely so heavily on financial support from the government.

Nowhere is political interference so well catalogued than in the history of the Olympic Games. Many games have been blighted by political statements or involvement. Here are some examples:

- ✪ *Antwerp 1920*: **None of the defeated nations from World War I were allowed to compete**
- ✪ *Berlin 1936*: **The German government used the games for Nazi propaganda**
- ✪ *Melbourne 1956*: **Spain and Holland withdrew due to the Soviet invasion of Hungary. Egypt and Lebanon did not compete as they were fighting for the Suez Canal. China withdrew as a protest over Taiwan's involvement in the games**
- ✪ *Tokyo 1964*: **South Africa was excluded due to apartheid after an all-white team were entered in the Rome games four years previously**
- ✪ *Mexico 1968*: **There were protests over government money spent on the games. Black American protests during medal ceremonies focused on the treatment of Black people in the USA**
- ✪ *Munich 1972*: **Israeli athletes and officials were killed and injured during a terrorist attack by Palestinian activists**
- ✪ *Montreal 1976*: **Many Black African nations boycotted the games**
- ✪ *Moscow 1980*: **The USA and many Western nations boycotted the games due to the poor record of the USSR on human rights and the invasion of Afghanistan in 1979**
- ✪ *Los Angles 1984*: **Many Eastern bloc countries boycotted the games on security grounds**
- ✪ *Barcelona 1992*: **South Africa returned to the games post apartheid and Germany fielded a single team after reunification. There was an ever present threat from Basque terrorists**
- ✪ *Atlanta 1996*: **Several spectators were killed in a bomb blast; right-wing activists were suspected**

Media in sport

The media – television, radio and newspapers – have had a tremendous effect on sport over the past few years. Increased coverage has contributed to sport's high profile in the UK. Tables 3.1 and 3.2 show the popularity of sport on TV.

Table 3.1   *TV sports programmes: the top 10 for 1997*

Event	Channel	Millions of viewers
Grand National	BBC1	15.16
FA Cup Final	BBC1	11.10
Man Utd v Porto	ITV	11.07
Man Utd v B Dortmund	ITV	10.77
Porto v Man Utd	ITV	10.32
B Dortmund v Man Utd	ITV	10.29
FA Cup: Man Utd v Spurs	BBC1	10.22
FA Cup: Chelsea v Liverpool	BBC1	9.98
Man Utd v Feyenoord	ITV	9.85
Feyenoord v Man Utd	ITV	9.68

Source   *Daily Telegraph* 17 January 1998

Table 3.2   *Non-football sporting events: television audiences for 1997*

Event	Millions of viewers
Five Nations Rugby	5.55
Wimbledon: finals weekend	5.25
British Grand Prix	5.02
Wimbledon: other play	3.51
The Derby	3.45
Rugby League Challenge Cup Final	2.71
Home Test Matches	2.26
Cheltenham Gold Cup	2.00

Source   House of Commons Written Answers 17 June 1998

Newspapers

There is a huge variety of newspaper sports coverage. The tabloids, such as the *Sun* or the *Mirror*, give a lot of space to sport, predominantly football and other popular competitions. Although they might disagree, their coverage often seems sensationalist and headline grabbing, focusing on contentious issues. The power of the tabloid press should not be underestimated. The campaign against Graham Taylor, depicted as a turnip when he was England football manager, accelerated his departure from the job.

The broadsheets, such as the *Times* or the *Independent*, dedicate less space to sport but try to cover a wider variety. The reporting is often analytical, quite unlike the tabloids. However, they can still spark controversy and debate; an excellent example is the *Times* interview given by Glen Hoddle when he was England manager. Hoddle's views on reincarnation and the comments he made about people with disabilities soon led to his resignation.

Radio

The popularity of sport has resulted in the first channel dedicated to sports coverage and related issues. Five Live broadcasts 24 hours a day with a mixture of sports and current affairs. Other stations, often local or regional, also cover sporting events.

Television

Television coverage of sport has increased dramatically over the years. The desire by people to witness great sporting achievements, whether live or recorded, has led to extensive exposure on the small screen. Such is the interest that cable television has three channels totally dedicated to sports coverage. Even the terrestrial channels are devoting much more time to sport.

Although the TV companies contribute large amounts of money to individual sports, their involvement is not always seen as a positive. Financial power held by TV has often been associated with the manipulation of sports to suit viewing times. TV companies have also been held responsible for the demise of some sports when coverage is reduced or ceased altogether. Here are two examples:

- **Moving football matches from traditional Saturdays to Sundays and Mondays**
- **Staging World Cup matches in the midday heat to obtain live coverage in Europe**

Cable television companies have recently tried to gain exclusive rights to cover the most popular sports in the country. By doing so they hope to increase sales of their subscriptions and the technology to receive their broadcasts. The

BSkyB has bought into English football
(Courtesy British Sky Broadcasting Ltd)

government, however, have identified certain events they call the Crown jewels, events such as Wimbledon, the FA Cup Final and the Grand National. These events must remain on terrestrial television and be accessible to the whole nation.

Activity 3.14

★ Research the viewing figures for the major sporting events over the past 10 years. What do the figures reveal?

★ List the technological advances made in television coverage over the years. Have they improved the sport or created problems for participants, officials and administrators?

★ What percentage of media coverage is dedicated to women's sport compared to male-dominated activities? How could the results affect future participation figures?

Working in the sports industry

The sports industry is one of the fastest-growing sectors of the economy and there are many job opportunities for people with the correct skills, knowledge, qualifications, attitude and personality.

Employment opportunities

The range of employment opportunities in sport is expanding all the time. Gone are the days when working in the sports industry was seen as 'not a proper job'. Today many rewarding, exciting and well-paid careers exist for correctly qualified, motivated, and above all, hard-working employees. The case study on page 130 looks at an organisation that offers a wide range of employment opportunities in sport. Meantime here is a more general overview.

Playing

Professional sportspeople have been around for a long time. Successful basketball, baseball and American football stars earn vast salaries in the USA, and although the types of reward may not be so high in the UK, many of the top Premiership players are reported to earn wages in excess of £10 000 per week. Here are some other sports in the UK where successful exponents can achieve a high standard of living:

- ✪ **Rugby union**
- ✪ **Rugby league**
- ✪ **Horse racing**
- ✪ **Snooker**
- ✪ **Golf**
- ✪ **Tennis**

Obviously, the rewards match the level of success achieved by participants and depend very heavily on the profile and financial standing of the sport.

Coaching

When they retire from competition, many sportspeople progress into coaching positions. This is very often down to a desire to put something back into the sport, or it can be seen as an extension of their playing career. Whatever the reason, coaching is being seen more and more as a viable career option for many people. Success on the playing field does not always mean success as a coach. There have been numerous examples where players who have reached the pinnacle in their sport have been unable to transfer this success into their coaching. Conversely, many mediocre players have made excellent coaches.

Management and administration

For sports enthusiasts without the desire to coach, a role in management or administration may be an attractive proposition. Management skills are much sought after in all sectors of the economy, and sport is no different. Efficient administrators are valuable to any organisation. The section on organisation and financing of sport in Unit 1 indicates the types of organisation where administrative positions exist.

Treatment of injury

Advances in medicine and treatment techniques have led to an increase in employment opportunities. All professional clubs will have an array of medical staff, perhaps including:

- ✪ **Doctor**
- ✪ **Physiotherapist**
- ✪ **Dietary consultant**
- ✪ **Sports psychologist**

Teaching

The expansion of sport has created a need for more teachers in the subject, from secondary school through to university. The range of qualifications now available require teachers to understand both academic and vocational aspects of sport. Coach education is also a growth area.

Sports development

The case study on Erewash Borough Council (page 111) exemplifies the growth of sports development positions throughout the UK. Sports development is a key priority at the moment and creates employment opportunities in:

- ✪ **Coaching**
- ✪ **Administration and coordination**
- ✪ **Coach education**

Retail

The explosion in the popularity of sportswear has produced a similar expansion in sports retailing. Every large town centre now seems to have a multitude of outlets selling a range of sports goods and accessories.

Promotion

Marketing is crucial to the success of any business, and sport is no different. There are positions within a range of sports organisations for people with promotional flair.

Gabby Yorath is a respected sports journalist
(Courtesy ITV Sport/On the Ball)

Media

With the explosion of sports coverage in the media, particularly radio and television, there are now many more employment opportunities. Once all the presenters were men but now there are several women presenters, such as Gabby Yorath.

Derby County Football Club

Derby County Football Club was formed as an offshoot of Derbyshire County Cricket Club in 1888. It has recently moved from its traditional home, the Baseball Ground, to a new purpose-built stadium at Pride Park on the outskirts of the city. Costing well over £20 million, the new stadium has been the catalyst for success both on and off the pitch. The club's turnover has almost doubled in a year, from £10.7 million in 1997 to just over £20 million in 1998. Derby County is big business. The club is now a seven day a week operation. In addition to its main function, providing football, its products and services include:

- ★ Conference and banqueting facilities
- ★ Behind-the-scenes tours
- ★ Match-day hospitality
- ★ Vision Rams – the club's own match-day TV service
- ★ Financial services, including credit services and insurance
- ★ Club superstores at the ground, city centre and East Midlands Airport

A club as large and diverse as Derby County offers a range of employment opportunities. Apart from the playing, management and coaching staff (82 full-time and 11 part-time) the club employs:

- ★ 32 full-time and 4 part-time ground staff, kitchen staff and cleaning staff
- ★ 77 full-time and 14 part-time administrative, retail and marketing staff

The total cost of wages and salaries amounts to over £10 million annually for the 200 plus staff at the club. All the positions on pages 127–8 exist at the club and at many more clubs throughout the football world.

The nature of the work

The millionaire lifestyle of many top sports performers portrays a glamorous and carefree existence, and although working in the industry is extremely enjoyable and rewarding, it is not always a bed of roses. Many jobs in the industry require an element of shift work, they require staff to work unsociable hours, including evenings and weekends, and they involve dealing with the public, including difficult and awkward customers. Besides these aspects, there may be others issues to consider; here are some of them.

Exercise 3.6

From the list of employment opportunities on pages 127–9, see how many require shift work and unsociable hours.

Part-time and casual work

Many jobs only offer part-time opportunities, although many staff see part-time work as an ideal medium for either progressing to full-time status or to see if they like the job in the first place. Many local authority leisure facilities rely heavily on part-time or casual staff to help provide cover at busy times of the day. Likewise many retail outlets have small numbers of staff on duty during the week but many more at weekends, when they are much busier.

Part-time employment does suit many people. Students find it beneficial as they can supplement their studies with much needed income as well as gaining valuable experience for later on. Working mums and dads who have responsibilities for school-age children also like the flexibility of part-time work.

Temporary and seasonal work

Unlike the tourism industry, the sports industry does not rely on a high percentage of seasonal and temporary employees. However, some jobs are only seasonal, which can present problems for people who need the security of an income all year round.

Think of some jobs in the sports industry that may be seasonal. Here are some examples to give you a start:

★ Gate staff at sports stadia

★ Security staff at the same venue

★ Coaches whose sport is seasonal

★ Seasonal sportspeople, e.g. professional cricketers

Many people overcome the problem of seasonal work by diversifying or by working in other sports or countries. Many football coaches work in the USA during the summer, and cricketers often play (or coach) for teams in South Africa and Australia.

The sought-after qualities

Whatever their position, employees in the sports industry will need certain skills, qualities, knowledge and technical abilities. Many careers allow for development on the job; there is no substitute for experience. Yet it's important to understand the basics before entering the industry. Every job has its own set of requirements, but below are some qualities that are useful in *most* sports jobs.

Not everyone is suited to working with the public. The public can be rude, aggressive and annoying; it requires a lot of patience to cope skilfully with difficult customers. The public can also be complimentary, generous and likeable; this makes the work rewarding and enjoyable. Consider these aspects of your personality:

- ✪ *Consistency*: **it is no good if your mood fluctuates with the weather**
- ✪ *Confidence*: **be able to talk to people and take control of situations**
- ✪ *Sense of humour*: **humour can defuse difficult situations or add to people's enjoyment**
- ✪ *Calmness*: **respond calmly to emergencies**
- ✪ *Employment skills*: **reliability, time management, punctuality, etc.**

What other skills do you think are important for sports employees? Do you possess them?

Many careers in sport will require specific technical knowledge and skill. A physiotherapist will need an excellent knowledge of anatomy, physiology, massage technique, rehabilitation, and so on.

The range of qualifications

The Department for Education and Employment has recently tried to streamline the system, but there are still a bewildering array of academic and vocational qualifications. It is crucial to choose correctly.

Academic qualifications

Academic qualifications are classed as those with 'theoretical' content. They are knowledge based and include:

- ✪ **GCSEs**
- ✪ **A-levels**
- ✪ **Degree programmes**
- ✪ **Masters awards**

Here are some examples of academic qualifications useful in the sports industry:

- ✪ **GCSE Physical Education**
- ✪ **A-level Sports Studies**
- ✪ **Degree in Sports Administration and Marketing**

These are only three examples of the academic qualifications available. Your local college, sixth-form school and university will be able to supply you with a more comprehensive list.

Vocational qualifications

Vocational qualifications have traditionally been available in occupations such as engineering and craft jobs. Until recently, sport was poorly represented in this area, despite the valiant efforts of professional bodies such as the Institute of

Sport and Recreation Management (ISRM) and the Institute of Leisure and Amenity Management (ILAM). Other educational awarding bodies (such as Edexcel) made provision in the form of first and national diplomas but it was rather sketchy.

All this changed with the advent of GNVQs (general national vocational qualifications) now known as Vocational A-levels if studied at Level 3 and NVQs (national vocational qualifications). The intention was to create parity of esteem between academic qualifications and vocational qualifications and to give employers and employees a clearly defined qualification structure.

The Vocational A-level covers a broad subject area, e.g. Leisure and Recreation, whereas an NVQ is more specific, e.g. Facility Operations. GNVQs at Level 2 or Vocational A-levels at Level 3 are predominantly tested through assignments and short tests, whereas NVQs are designed for the workplace and can be tested by practical competence.

Governing bodies and other sports-related bodies also add to the range of vocational qualifications. Table 3.3 gives an overview of the vocational qualifications currently available within sport.

Table 3.3 *Some vocational qualifications in sport*

GNVQ/National/ Higher	NVQ	Governing body	Others
Leisure & Recreation	Operational Services	ISRM – Operators' Certificate	RLSS – NPLQ
Sport Science	No equivalence	No equivalence	No equivalence
Outdoor Education	Coaching, Teaching & Instructing	British Canoe Union awards	NCFE – Preparation for entry to the outdoor industry
Exercise & Fitness	Coaching, Teaching & Instructing	As NVQ	RSA – Exercise to music

All the qualifications in Table 3.3 are available at different levels. All governing bodies are striving to align their qualifications within the NVQ framework. All GNVQs and NVQs have key skills embedded within their framework

An increasingly influential body in the sports industry is SPRITO (full title National Training Organisation for Sport Recreation and Allied Occupations). SPRITO represents:

- ✪ **Sport and recreation**
- ✪ **Playwork**
- ✪ **Outdoor education**
- ✪ **Fitness and exercise**

It has a responsibility to develop vocational qualifications in these four areas; the qualifications are then sanctioned by the Qualifications and Curriculum Authority (QCA). Two major developments by SPRITO have been national traineeships and modern apprenticeships, in line with other sectors of the economy. Both are proving popular with employers and employees alike. Traineeships are designed for employees at operational level, and apprenticeships are aimed at supervisory level.

Activity 3.15

Have you identified your next step? Will it be straight into employment or does it involve further study? A good starting point would be to contact your local careers advisor, who will help you prepare a career action plan. Once you have read the next section you will be in a better position to plan your next move. Do not leave it too late.

The ways to get jobs

How do you go about landing your dream job? One thing's for sure, it's not going to be easy. For a start, gaining the correct qualifications will take plenty of study and hard work. Then you have to pit yourself against many other candidates, all eyeing the same vacancy.

Unit 1 will tell you all you need to know about writing CVs, completing application forms, attending interviews, etc. This section looks more specifically at where you might find the job you've been looking for.

Newspapers

Many local and national papers have regular job features and employment pages. It's a good idea to find out when most jobs are advertised, e.g. Wednesday, and make sure you check out that paper each week. If buying the paper is a problem, your local library might have a copy. It is important to act quickly. There is nothing more frustrating than missing a deadline or applying when the vacancy has been filled.

The National Training Organisation for
Sport Recreation & Allied Occupations

Sport & Recreation
Playwork
Outdoor Education &
Development Training
Fitness & Exercise

MODERN APPRENTICESHIPS

Study: NEWARK & SHERWOOD DISTRICT COUNCIL

The Organisation

Newark & Sherwood District Council is located in the heart of Nottingham. The Council operates 7 Leisure Centres from its Leisure Services Department. This case study concentrates primarily on Southwell Leisure Centre which is a charitable trust financially supported by Newark & Sherwood District Council. The leisure centre provides a valuable community facility for all including extensive use by many local schools, a venue for private sports clubs and special events such as arts and craft fairs and various courses ranging from swimming to football. Southwell Leisure Centre has a workforce of 35, 7 full time and 28 part time workers, and as a member of SPRITO is committed to the training and development of all their staff.

Background to Modern Apprenticeships

Newark and Sherwood's work with MAs began in 1996 in the Southwell Leisure Centre. The council now has four leisure centres operating Modern Apprenticeships (MAs) in Sport and Recreation. The Council sees the MA programme as a great success that has made a valuable contribution to its human resource strategy. A total of 30 young people have been involved in the MA. 10 of those have now successfully completed the programme, and 6 have been promoted from Leisure Attendant to Duty Officer.

Commitment

Daphne James, the Centre Manager and NVQ Co-ordinator at the time, explains why Southwell chose to introduce MAs.

'Modern Apprenticeships provided us with an ideal progression route for our Level 2 NVQ candidates into facility supervision and management. This gave us the opportunity to train and develop staff on the broader aspects of the industry and the running of a modern leisure centre.'

The centre strongly believed that MAs would build on and improve Southwell's training strategy, motivate its staff and improve overall performance. As a charitable trust supported by the Council, approval was needed from the Board of Trustees to introduce the MA.

'Commitment and support at strategic and management level is vital to the success of any training and development programme', says Daphne.

The Route Taken

Since the Centre already delivered NVQs, preparing for the introduction of MAs was made easier since the people and systems needed were already in place.

'We had already developed strong partnership links with the local college and the North Nottinghamshire Training and Enterprise Council (TEC) and were well known for our quality delivery of NVQs.'

The TEC agreed to contract directly with Southwell so that the funding to pay for the Apprentices' training would go directly to the Centre. Newark and Sherwood College was on hand to act as approved centre, and provide training in the knowledge for the NVQs and some of the Key Skills needed for the MA. The overall work of introducing the MA was guided by a Steering Group, and a lot of care was taken to make sure that there were clearly agreed responsibilities for all those involved in delivering the programme.

24 Stephenson Way, London, NW1 2HD

Tel: 0171 388 7755   Fax: 0171 388 9733   Email:the.nto@sprito.org.uk

SPRITO offers modern apprenticeships and national traineeships
(Courtesy SPRITO)

The National Training Organisation for
Sport Recreation & Allied Occupations

Sport & Recreation
Playwork
Outdoor Education &
Development Training
Fitness & Exercise

NATIONAL TRAINEESHIPS

Study: COTSWOLD LEISURE CENTRE

The Organisation

The Cotswold Leisure Centre is run as an in-house contract with Cotswold District Council. It comprises of a swimming pool, sports hall, activity room, squash courts catering facility and a health & Fitness suite with spa and sunbed facilities. As the main leisure centre for what is a predominately rural area, it has a catchment area of approximately 75,000 and attracts people from all corners of the Cotswolds and North Wiltshire, with over 400,000 customers a year and is used by over 40 school groups. Cotswold Leisure Centre employs 94 staff, 22 full-time and approximately 72 casual workers.

Background to National Traineeships

Cotswold Leisure Centre was already involved in the delivery of Modern Apprenticeships which focussed the centres original training towards NVQ standards. Therefore when National Traineeships were introduced it was a natural step for the centre to take.

Fiona Hibbard, Duty Manager explains:

'We already have 2 Modern Apprentices working towards Sport & Recreation NVQs with Gayton Consultancy and Training, so when they mentioned National Traineeships, we welcomed it with open arms.'

National Traineeships were first introduced at Cotswold Leisure Centre in January 1998 as part of a pilot with Gloucestershire TEC testing the integration of key skills in the work place and a 'paperless portfolio' approach.

Commitment

The Cotswold Leisure Centre is very committed to the training and development of its staff, in May 1997 the centre was re-accredited as an 'Investor in People'. All employees are involved in some form of training from short courses, coaching awards, NVQs, Apprenticeships/Traineeships to external college courses.

Cotswold Leisure Centre felt that a work-based qualification for their employees would provide an opportunity for some staff to achieve a qualification who would not always be suited to a more formal approach.

'We hope to see that National Traineeships improve motivation and self-confidence in our younger members of staff, giving a more committed workforce with a recognised qualification'

Cotswold Leisure Centre is an accredited 'Investors in People' and believes that National Traineeships fit well within the organisations delivery of training and development to sustain this standard.

The Route Taken

Since Cotswold Leisure Centre already delivered Modern Apprenticeships, the introduction of National Traineeships was a simple task since the majority of people and systems were already in place.

'We already worked successfully with Gayton Consultancy and Training and were supported by Gloucestershire TEC for delivery of Modern Apprenticeships

The implementation of National Traineeships followed on from the already successful work of Modern Apprenticeships in partnership with Gayton and support from the TEC. Gayton trained up three in-house assessors at the Leisure Centre and together worked in partnership to build training and assessment into everyday work activities.

'Assessment takes place when the candidate and assessors feel the time is appropriate and is integrated into the candidates shift pattern. Additional key skills training is carried out on a one to one basis with the candidate in-house to fit into the candidates everyday work programme, with operational issues in mind we always find this approach successful."

24 Stephenson Way, London, NW1 2HD
Tel: 0171 388 7755   Fax: 0171 388 9733   Email:the.nto@sprito.org.uk

CASE STUDY... CASE STUDY... CASE STUDY... CASE STUDY...

Magazines

The sports industry has a range of dedicated magazines. Publications such as *Leisure News*, *The Great Outdoors* and *Fitness First* all carry interesting editorial and plenty of situations vacant.

Careers advisors

People often think that careers advisors cater only for school and college leavers. This is not true. They will offer advice and guidance to anyone and they often have up-to-date information on initiatives and schemes that may suit you.

Other organisations such as the Training and Enterprise Councils (TECs) can also help with advice and possible financial support. The Southern Derbyshire Chamber is currently running a scheme that contributes up to £150 towards training costs.

Training initiatives

Employment agencies will also help you find work. Registering your availability may just pay off. Other options include:

- **Job fairs**
- **Speculative letters**
- **Word of mouth**

Many jobs not only require qualifications and personal qualities but also demand relevant work experience. Make sure this does not let you down. If part-time work is not available in your chosen area, ensure the work you do take involves some of these aspects:

- ★ Working with people
- ★ Involvement with health and safety
- ★ Working unsociable hours

Activity 3.16

Skim your local press for suitable sports jobs then request application forms and/or further details. It does not matter if you are not serious about the job because the information you receive can go into a portfolio for future reference. This should give you a good idea about what to expect when you start applying for real.

Further information

UK Sport
Walkden House
3–10 Melton Street
London NW1 2EB

020 7380 8000
www.uksportscouncil.co.uk

Sport England
16 Upper Woburn Place
London WC1H 0QP

020 7273 1500
www.english.sports.gov.uk

Revision questions

1 What are the three families of sport?

2 Briefly describe how sport has developed over the ages.

3 Give a brief definition of the word 'sport'.

4 How can participation in sport benefit individuals?

5 In many schools the opportunity to participate in sport has greatly diminished. Why is this?

6 What are the responsibilities of international sports federations (ISFs)?

7 What are the three main policy areas of Sport England?

8 Briefly summarise the Let's Kick Racism out of Football campaign.

9   How has political influence affected the Olympic Games over the years?

10 What are quangos and what do they do?

11 How has the National Lottery benefited sport since its introduction?

12 How has the media influenced the sports industry in recent years?

13 Name the six national sports centres and say which sports they focus on.

14 Briefly summarise employment opportunities in the sports industry.

15 What sort of personal qualities would you expect of someone employed in the sports industry?

Marketing

4

Objectives

- **Define marketing**
- **Describe and explain the principles of marketing in leisure and recreation**
- **Describe and explain market research**
- **Appreciate the role of communication in marketing**
- **Apply all of these to the leisure and recreation industry**

Marketing is all about the customer; it is an important and structured part of any business that concentrates on the needs of the customer and then the supply of a product or service to meet these needs. It also looks at the presentation of these products or services in the right way, at the right time, in the right place and at the right price. Because marketing studies the customer in some detail, it is very closely linked with customer service (Unit 5) and also the optional unit on human resources. To get the full picture, read this unit alongside Unit 5.

Definitions of marketing

Whatever your role in the leisure and recreation industry, you need to understand the significance of **marketing**. Marketing is:

✪ **About the customer**

✪ **Planning and organising a business to meet the needs of the customer**

✪ **Often driven by money**

✪ **Part of an overall business plan**

✪ **A major planning exercise that when carried out effectively should lead to financial reward**

✪ **A continuous process**

✪ **A way of approaching a business that will affect everyone connected with the business**

✪ **Not persuading the customer to buy something they do not want**

✪ **A way to success (but with no guarantees)**

✪ **Not to be glanced at and disregarded**

Marketing leisure and recreation

When you have looked at customer service in Unit 5, you will see that marketing and customer service have similar backgrounds. In fact, the two seem to have developed together. This is not really surprising when they have so much in common and the same focus – the customer. Marketing is now considered important in all sectors of the leisure and recreation industry.

The private sector has concentrated a great deal of time and effort on marketing. A marketing department or a marketing manager is almost always identified in private sector organisations. Effective marketing is considered important because it increases sales and profits, making more money for the organisation.

In the public sector, the value of marketing was not readily recognised. This has changed over the past 20 years. The public sector concentrated almost solely on providing a service to everyone in the community. The financial details of local authority leisure services were not so well scrutinised as the private sector. The numbers of customers using a facility did not directly relate to income or profit. In the public sector a drop in the number of customers would seldom close down a facility, whereas closure was much more likely in the private sector. The financial aims of the public sector were quite low on the list of priorities.

In the 1980s this changed with the introduction of compulsory competitive tendering and, more recently, best value. This introduced much closer financial control and viability. The public sector was forced to look at what services it provided and if they were worthwhile to the community and to the accountants. The customer was suddenly seen in a different light, as a measure of success or failure, just as it has always been in the private sector.

The public sector was being made to compete and to adopt the principles of private sector management. Marketing was one of these principles. Marketing has therefore become a more recognisable function in the public sector and there are now employment opportunities at all levels.

The voluntary sector has also changed its way of working in recent years. A major influence has been the introduction of the National Lottery. Charitable and voluntary organisations have always relied heavily on people's donations and subscriptions in order to survive. These have fallen since the National Lottery was introduced as people see part of this money going to 'good causes', including the leisure and recreation industry. Maybe we prefer to gamble on becoming a millionaire.

Many smaller organisations have suffered as a result of these changes. Consequently, voluntary groups have to compete against each other for the money that is available. The money can often go to the group that shouts the loudest and makes themselves heard. This has increased the importance of marketing in the voluntary sector.

Paid marketing positions are frequently advertised in the voluntary sector. In small voluntary clubs, such as a local swimming club, marketing is an identified function along with the secretary, treasurer and chairperson. Organisations within the voluntary sector have realised they are in a competitive industry, so they have started to market their products and services more aggressively than in the past.

Marketing objectives

Marketing objective
a statement that specifies what an organisation wants to achieve within a certain period of time; these statements are specific to marketing.

Decide on your **marketing objectives** then think how to achieve them. They can relate to the marketing department, the marketing function or the marketing manager. As with any objective, they should be:

- ✪ **Accompanied by deadlines**
- ✪ **Clear and measurable**
- ✪ **Realistic and achievable**
- ✪ **Agreed by all relevant parties**

○ **Cover all timescales**

short, medium, long

Here is a poorly written objective:

The aim of Newtown Leisure Centre is to reduce admission prices.

This does not state which prices will go down, when they will go down and how much they will go down. Here is a more useful marketing objective:

Swimming admission charges at Newtown Leisure Centre will be reduced by 10% from January 2001.

This states which prices will be reduced, how much they will be reduced and when the reduction will begin. Marketing objectives are likely to be relevant in any aspect of an organisation that involves the customer. Here are some possible areas:

○ *Pricing*: **to reduce prices for ski hire by 8% in 2002**

○ *Location and distribution*: **to open five new outlets in out-of-city locations by 2000**

○ *Customer service*: **the telephone will be answered within four rings**

○ *Promotions*: **special discount rates**

○ *Sales targets*: **ten gold membership packages are to be sold every week**

○ *Market share*: **to increase market share by 5% in 2001 (market share is an organisation's share of the total market)**

○ *Target markets*: **to attract 200 new customers from the 18–30 age group (target markets are certain types of customer that products are aimed at)**

Influential factors

○ **The overall objectives of a particular organisation. A private health club may make their main objectives money and profit. A public or non-commercial organisation may focus on participation rates and be less concerned with sales targets in relation to profit**

○ **How long the organisation has been established. To make an impact, a new company may need greater promotion and advertising in its first year than in subsequent years**

○ **The product life cycle (page 157). If a product is relaunched, it may need a greater marketing thrust**

○ **External and internal influences (page 152)**

The marketing process

Once we have decided our objectives, it is time to think how we are going to achieve them. To satisfy the customer and make ourselves a profit, we need to develop a plan. This plan needs to be logical and structured. It is usually split into four stages:

1 **Identify customer needs**

2 **Develop a product or service**

3 **Communicate with the customer**

4 **Evaluate how it went**

This process never stops; it is continual and dynamic. We can always improve what we do, and the customer is always changing their mind about their needs. To make improvements, we must evaluate what we do then refine it to meet the customer's needs more closely.

THE MARKETING PROCESS

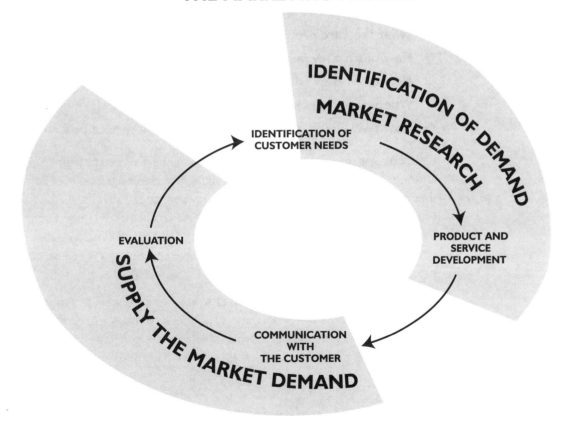

REMEMBER THIS IS DYNAMIC AND CONTINUOUS

The marketing process usually divides into four stages

Stage 1: Identify customer needs

Link   page 196

Types of customer

Through a variety of methods in Unit 5, an organisation can state with some certainty and accuracy what a customer wants. This is the part of the process that deals with demand. An organisation must find out exactly what its customers want; it mustn't guess what they want or try to tell them what they want. If you don't know what the customer wants, it is difficult to provide it. Then your products could fail to sell, your profits could go down and you could go bankrupt.

This stage of the marketing process is sometimes disregarded. Some marketeers are too arrogant or too ignorant to identify the needs of the customer. For example, someone thinks they have a great idea, they are full of enthusiasm, they spend large amounts of money producing a product or service, then they find it wasn't wanted at all. By this stage money has been lost. If it was your money, wouldn't you wish you had stopped, thought about it and then spent it wisely? It can be a high price to pay for overenthusiasm. So by the end of the first stage, an organisation needs an accurate picture of:

- ✪ **Who their customer will be**
- ✪ **What their needs and expectations are**
- ✪ **What they are prepared to pay**
- ✪ **How much they are likely to buy and spend**
- ✪ **How often they will buy it**
- ✪ **Where they will buy it from**
- ✪ **How they would like to see the product or service presented**

Let's look at an example. In order to provide the best service to their customers, Girl Power Go for It health and fitness club have found out that their customers are mainly overweight, body conscious and unfit. As the name suggests, they are all female. These customers identify that it is important that the facility is clean, attractive, warm, easy to get to and unintimidating to people of all body shapes. Most customers have children under 12 years of age.

Customer needs should be prioritised as some are more significant than others. The colour of the packaging may not be very important, but then again it might be. Remember it is impossible to provide the perfect service for everyone but the more relevant information we have, the more likely we are to get it right.

Stage 2: Develop a product or service

Now we know what the customer wants, we need to go ahead and provide it. This part of the process deals with supply. Using the information collected, a product or service can be developed that is:

- ✪ **What the customer wants**
- ✪ **Priced at the appropriate level**
- ✪ **Available where the customer wants to buy it**
- ✪ **Packaged in a way that attracts the customer**

The Girl Power Go for It health and fitness club offers a service to females only. There are no mirrors in the exercise rooms; there are services that address diet and fitness together and there is nursery provision and an after-school club. There is also ample car parking close by. Members of staff wear conservative dress, not leotards and thongs.

Stage 3: Communicate with the customer

The customer now has a service that is just what they are looking for; in other words, supply matches demand. Now we need to ensure the customer knows about the product or service on offer. How to create this awareness will be covered later on in the sections on Marketing Mix and Marketing Communications. However, let's continue with Girl Power Go for It and consider the best ways of telling the customer what's on offer. Here are some suggestions:

- ✪ **Local radio adverts and free feature packages**
- ✪ **A flyer in all free local papers delivered in the local catchment area**
- ✪ **A no-obligation 'have a go' day**
- ✪ **Leaflets and promotions in the local shopping centres**

> Tell the target customer what's on sale and relate it to what they asked for. Don't invite someone to improve their cardiovascular efficiency, encourage them to look good for their summer holiday

Stage 4: Evaluate how it went

If all things have gone well so far, we'll have a product that's in demand and a customer who knows about it. If we've got this right, the chances of success are high. However, our likes and dislikes change over time. What we once thought was brilliant we now think is just alright. And in Girl Power Go for It what happens to the overweight, unfit women when they are not overweight and unfit? Identification of customer needs has to start all over again, to ensure the service continues to meet the customer's needs – the supply continues to meet the demand. An evaluation can be carried out in many ways, including:

- ✪ **Customer suggestion boxes**
- ✪ **Focus groups**

- ❂ **Informal feedback**
- ❂ **Questionnaires**
- ❂ **Sales figures**

As with many processes that are completed in a changing environment, they need to be repeated and reviewed regularly. In most instances the marketing process should be completed yearly. There may be reasons for completing it more often and these can include:

- ❂ **A recession**
- ❂ **A drop in sales figures**
- ❂ **A rise in customer complaints**
- ❂ **Useful customer suggestions**
- ❂ **Competition**

Activity 4.1

Think of two leisure and recreation products, services, activities or venues. Just as we have done for Girl Power Go for It, apply each stage of the marketing process to your chosen topics. Compare the two facilities, identifying similarities and differences. This time go one stage further. If you were in charge, what would you do differently and why?

Market segmentation

Sometimes when we are applying the marketing process, we decide it would be useful to look more closely at our customers and try to segment the market. Closely linked with the customer types in Unit 5, segmentation is based on the idea that various customer sectors want, need or value similar qualities from a product, these sectors can be identified as segments and these segments can be targeted by different products.

The aim of **market segmentation** is to identify a relational classification by linking a particular group of customers and then creating an awareness of a product or service targeted at this particular group. This process aims to allow an organisation to pay close attention to the needs of the customer and to apply its thrust as effectively as possible. Hopefully this will encourage a customer to return time and time again.

Consider this aim carefully. If there is no reason for segmentation or classifying the customer then don't do it. It may be that a segment of the population has size 12 feet, this may be of no relevance to the restaurateur but may be significant to the bowling alley when buying in bowling shoes for hire. There are many ways of classifying or segmenting the customer:

- ✪ **Age**
- ✪ **Sex**
- ✪ **Nationality**
- ✪ **Income or wealth**
- ✪ **Occupation**

These types are discussed in depth in Unit 5. However, there are some standard classification methods in marketing:

- ✪ *The family life cycle* (**Table 4.1**): **This process may be a useful tool when classifying leisure activities through our lives, but it is only a guide and some groups of people don't fit anywhere. It is also a rather traditional view of life. Not everyone gets married, has children, works all their life and then dies alone**

- ✪ *Classification by occupation and wealth* (**Table 4.2**): **This too is a useful guide with some gaps, e.g. people that don't need to work. Social class is supposed to be a thing of the past, but this classification may still be relevant**

- ✪ *Classification by customer behaviour* (**Table 4.3**): **The way we behave as customers can be used to help with marketing. Skimmed milk is often packaged in cartons featuring athletes or slim women; this is targeting customers who desire to be fit and slim. Buy now, pay later products target customers who make a purchase then think how to afford it**

Table 4.1 *The family life cycle*

Stage in family life cycle	Comments
Bachelor	Young and single
Newly married	Young, no children
Full nest 1	Youngest child under 6
Full nest 2	Youngest child over 6
Full nest 3	Children still at home but working
Empty nest 1	One partner working; children left home
Empty nest 2	Both partners retired
Solitary survivor 1	Still at work
Solitary survivor 2	Retired

Table 4.2 *Classifying customers by occupation and wealth*

Social grade	Social class	Job type	Salary (£)	Job in the leisure industry
A	Upper middle	Director, owner	>45 000	Chief executive of a private health club
B	Middle	Manager	25 000	Leisure centre (LC) manager LC personnel manager LC marketing manager
C1	Lower middle	Supervisor	16 000	LC duty officer LC marketing officer LC assistant manager
C2	Skilled working	Manual	14 000	Technician Lifeguard
D	Working	Manual	7 000	Cleaner
E	Subsistence	Manual or non-working	<7 000	Odd-job person Casual worker

Table 4.3 *Classifying customers by behaviour*

Influence on behaviour	Comment
Price	Customers that seek bargains
Material goods	Customers that buy now and think later
Quality	Customers that seek value for money
Loyal customers	Customers that buy out of loyalty
Lifestyle	Customers that buy on their beliefs and desires

Segmentation: a step-by-step guide

1   **Identify the specific product, service or focus**
2   **Identify the segments**
3   **Validate them; are the segments accurate?**
4   **Select the target customers**
5   **Develop marketing strategies for the target customers**
6   **Monitor progress and make any changes**

Exercise 4.1

Look at yourself and your friends:

★ Identify any common characteristics or interests; these are your segments

★ Identify segments that may be useful in the leisure and recreation industry

★ Consider these segments and discuss products and services that may be targeted at you

Influential factors

▼▼▼▼▼▼▼▼▼

External factors
influences that occur outside the organisation and that the organisation has little or no control over

Internal factors
influences that occur inside the organisation and that can be controlled by the organisation

▲▲▲▲▲▲▲▲▲▲

A competitive, forward-thinking business will be able to look at itself in an objective fashion. It will understand the factors that can influence success or failure, both **external factors** and **internal factors**. Here are some of them:

Table 4.4 *External factors and how they influence marketing*

External factor	Effect on any business	Effect on leisure businesses
National economy		
Rise in interest rates	Customers will have reduced disposable income; they won't be able to spend so much after paying the bills	Leisure can be seen as a luxury purchase; people usually cut their leisure spending before they cut the essentials
Reduction in interest rates	Customers will have increased disposable income	This could increase the number of customers
Employment trends	High unemployment	Increase in off-peak customers and more people on concessions
	Low unemployment	High level of peak use; more customers will have money to spend on health clubs, holidays, etc.
Demographics		
Age, sex, wealth, etc.	Different customer types	Provide a service that is in demand by the specific types of customer in the local area, e.g. activities for parents and toddlers where there are many young families
Competitors		
A rival organisation sets up business nearby	Customers may be curious about the new business, switching purchases and then perhaps their loyalty	Remain competitive by trying to keep existing customers and attracting new customers

- ✪ **The size of the organisation**
- ✪ **The aims of the organisation**
- ✪ **The philosophy of the organisation**
- ✪ **The qualifications of the staff**
- ✪ **Staff development, professional and personal**

All factors have the same ultimate effect; they can change the behaviour of the customer, which can affect sales and profit.

Let's look at the external factors in Table 4.4, and remember, the key to success is to adapt the management process for 'identifying, anticipating and satisfying requirements of the customer'.

The external factors in Table 4.4 are often analysed using marketing tools. Here an appropriate tool is a PEST analysis to help determine future strategies.

P = political factors
E = economic factors
S = social factors and
T = technological factors

Table 4.5 *How to conduct a PEST analysis*

Political	Economic	Social
Government policy	High interest rates	Organisation sponsored an out-of-school sports club during the early evenings
Local elections in the next year	High levels of unemployment	
Change in child benefit		
Emphasis on sporting excellence		
Introduction of best value		
Technological	**Environmental**	**Other**
Internets and intranets	Recycling promotion	New rival opening in six months
Web marketing	Energy-saving plan	
	Noise problems in the evenings and noise from a generator in the plant room	

Other factors to consider are environmental factors and competition. A PEST analysis is usually carried out by senior staff involved in the direction and focus of the organisation. These are the people who make decisions and plan for the future.

It is always best that more than one person carries out this analysis, as one person alone cannot analyse every piece of information accurately. Having more than one person will help to minimise error and build a more accurate representation of the external factors. A useful way to conduct a PEST analysis is to use a grid (Table 4.5).

The key to success is not just to collect and analyse the information, but to act upon it. If a rival organisation is opening nearby in the next six months, think how you will retain your customers and how you will retain your staff. Plan a campaign to minimise any disruption from the rival's opening.

Now let's look at the internal factors in Table 4.6; these too are often analysed with marketing tools. Here an appropriate tool is SWOT analysis:

S = strengths
W = weaknesses
O = opportunities
T = threats

In this case, unlike PEST analysis, it is not just the strategic or decision-making staff that complete the analysis. It is useful to ask members of staff from all levels and parts of an organisation; get as many as possible to complete it. The

Table 4.6   *Internal factors and how they influence marketing*

Internal factor	Effect on any business	Effect on leisure businesses
Does the organisation recognise the importance of marketing?	If no, then nobody does the job	Customers may not know about the organisation
Does the organisation study the needs of the customer?	If no, these needs are unlikely to be met, so there may be a reduction in customer numbers	Activities may suffer poor attendance or low numbers of participants
	If yes, this should give an increase in customer numbers through new and repeat business	Increased demand for popular activities
Pricing strategies	Prices are too high or too low	Customers can see a product as a rip-off or as not worth buying

Table 4.7 *How to carry out a SWOT analysis*

Strengths	Weaknesses
Excellent GCSE grades	Poor time management
Working part-time at a local leisure centre	Bus is always late on a Monday, so I miss the first part of Investigating Leisure and Recreation
I like the teachers	
I enjoy using IT	

Opportunities	Threats
Helping me develop my career prospects	Lack of money
Looking at going to university	No computer at home
I've enjoyed marketing so much, I'd like to specialise in it later on	Limited internet access, so it's hard to gather information

SWOT analysis should be completed for all areas separately and then for the organisation as a whole.

A senior manager should carefully analyse these comments, as many great ideas originate from people most closely involved with the product or service. Also, by asking all staff to complete this process, you are showing them that you value their opinions. This can be an excellent way to motivate and empower a team. A useful way to conduct a SWOT analysis is to use a grid (Table 4.7), as we did with the PEST analysis. As an example, look at a SWOT analysis for you and your Vocational A-level.

Nothing is perfect, and to succeed in your studies you have to plan, compromise and do the best you can. Exactly the same is true at work. Be aware of the pressures, maximise your strengths and minimise your weaknesses. At the end of this unit you will look at two case studies then complete a PEST analysis and a SWOT analysis.

The marketing mix

The **marketing mix** includes the four P's:

- ✪ **Product**
- ✪ **Place**

Marketing mix

a collection of variables that an organisation can identify, manipulate and change to achieve a certain level of sales or targets

Product

the actual item or service that is on sale; the thing the customer will buy or experience

Branding

products with a set of common characteristics that make them distinctive from their rivals. This branding can be a logo, e.g. the Virgin logo. It can be colour identification, e.g. the purple chocolate wrapping of Cadbury. It can be music, e.g. the 'Eastenders' theme tune. Whatever it is, it has to be simple, short and instantly recognisable.

- ✪ **Price**
- ✪ **Promotion**

as well as other variables:

- ✪ **People**
- ✪ **Politics**
- ✪ **The environment**
- ✪ **Technology**

The successful organisation will study these variables to produce a marketing strategy for achieving their specified objectives.

Product

Here are some aspects and characteristics to consider:

- ✪ **Features of the product**
- ✪ **Quality**
- ✪ **Packaging**
- ✪ **The name of the product**
- ✪ **Branding**
- ✪ **After-sales**

When a product or service is launched, it needs to be comprehensively researched to ensure the customer wants to buy it in the first place. A product must be in demand, as without this demand there is no one to buy it. This is called product or market research and development.

Branding and logos: Derby County chose a ram
(Courtesy Derby County Football Club)

Table 4.8 *Life cycles for products and humans*

Product life cycle	Human life cycle
Idea	Conception
Development	Pregnancy
Launch	Birth
Growth	Childhood, puberty
Maturity	Young adulthood
Saturation	Middle age
Decline	Old age
Elimination	Death

The demand and appeal of certain products change over time. This can be linked to influences such as technological development, new brands, varying economic conditions and competition. When there are changes in demand, it is up to the organisation to react to them so the success of the product can be continued.

▼ ▼ ▼ ▼ ▼ ▼ ▼ ▼ ▼

Product life cycle
the stages in a product's life

▲ ▲ ▲ ▲ ▲ ▲ ▲ ▲ ▲

The **product life cycle** may be compared with our own life cycle and described as a series of changes (Table 4.8). All products follow this life cycle but over different periods of time. Some products remain popular for decades, others are launched and die very quickly. The secret of the PLC is

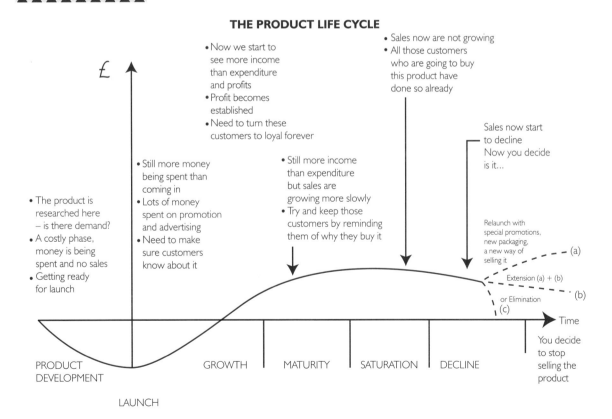

THE PRODUCT LIFE CYCLE

Products have a life cycle rather like ours

A VARIETY OF PRODUCT LIFE CYCLES

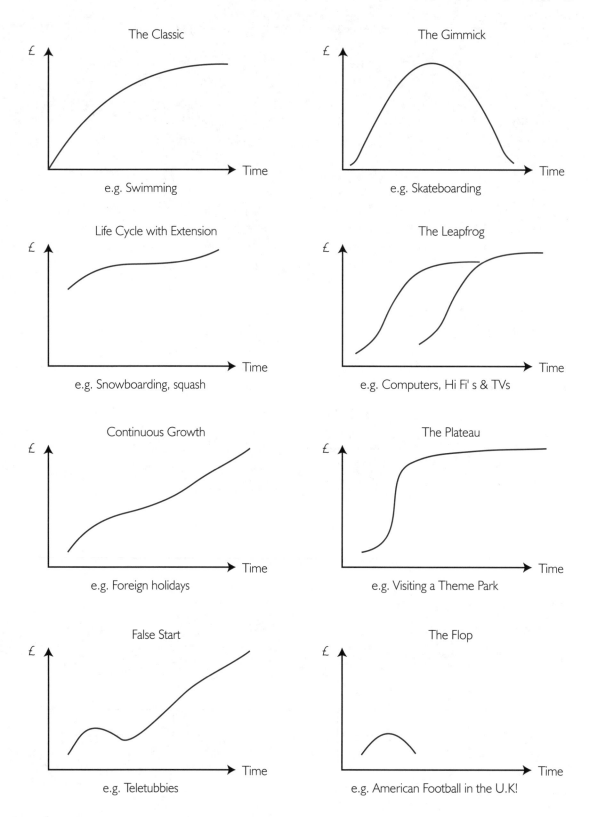

The Classic

£ / Time

e.g. Swimming

The Gimmick

£ / Time

e.g. Skateboarding

Life Cycle with Extension

£ / Time

e.g. Snowboarding, squash

The Leapfrog

£ / Time

e.g. Computers, Hi Fi' s & TVs

Continuous Growth

£ / Time

e.g. Foreign holidays

The Plateau

£ / Time

e.g. Visiting a Theme Park

False Start

£ / Time

e.g. Teletubbies

The Flop

£ / Time

e.g. American Football in the U.K!

Graphing money versus time gives curves that you can recognise

to recognise the progression of the product and apply marketing strategies to keep the product in the most desirable phase. This is known as extending the product life cycle.

Page 158 shows a variety of product life cycles and types of product. A successful organisation needs a mixture of product types. It needs safe, reliable products – classics – that have steady sales and help to pay the wages. It needs new products with the potential to become classics. It needs products that are very popular very quickly and bring in lots of money in a short time – gimmicks. It doesn't need products that no one buys – flops. Organisations should try to analyse all their products in one go. There are marketing tools that do this, e.g. the Boston matrix.

> Take a step back to analyse the products and services you sell. You may have a wonderful window display and efficient staff but customers do not want to buy your services because they are out of date. Continually review your performance and analyse what you are actually selling.

Exercise 4.2

Go through the product life cycles on page 158 and replace each example with a different one. Try to pick products from the leisure and recreation industry. As a group, discuss these products then choose the most well-known example of each.

Consider the flop and the gimmick. How could you extend their product life cycles? Select some successful brands from leisure and recreation. Identify the logo, theme tune or slogan that makes each brand recognisable. Show them to your friends and ask them to name the product. See how easily they can do it.

Place

Place is another important variable within the marketing mix. It refers to the physical location of a product or service and also the method of distribution – how the product gets to the customer.

Location

Location is central to success. Whatever you're selling, sell it in the right location. For example, an expensive, exclusive and luxurious health spa, offering first-class accommodation, is best suited to an exclusive country location, not an inner-city area plagued by high crime levels and deprivation. Here are some aspects to consider:

- ✪ **Attractiveness**
- ✪ **Accessibility**
- ✪ **Mobility**
- ✪ **Awareness**

    Will customers know of the site?

    Is it on a main road?

    Is it seen by passers-by every day?

- ✪ **Adaptability**

    Can the location change as your products change?

- ✪ **Room for expansion**
- ✪ **Political, economic and financial constraints**

    Cost of land

    Rent of an outlet

- ✪ **Competition**

    Consider the locations of any rivals

    Don't site yourself too near a competitor

- ✪ **The location of customers to the site**
- ✪ **The customer profile**

    Locate close to your target customers

Sometimes it is difficult to find the perfect site; at some point you need to prioritise the aspects you consider the most important then compromise on the location you choose. For example, if we all had as much money as we wanted, we would probably live in a different house, but money governs the home we can live in. This is the same when choosing a location for a business. Aim to maximise sales of your products and services.

Distribution

Distribution enables the customer to buy a product or service, perhaps in a shop or through a catalogue. All products need a sales outlet, so distribution is important. Choose your method carefully. Distribution is expensive and you want to spend your money wisely. It is also where many customers form their first impressions and you want them to be good. Here are four reasons to consider distribution:

- ✪ **It creates a purchase opportunity – somewhere for the product to be bought**
- ✪ **It provides a service opportunity – somewhere the customer can assess the suitability of the product, have the product serviced, maintained and repaired**
- ✪ **It promotes the product; the outlet for distribution can create public awareness through window displays, etc.**
- ✪ **It plays a social role; the distribution outlet becomes part of a locality, e.g. a leisure centre can become the focal point of a community**

Methods of distribution include:

- ✪ **Shops**
- ✪ **Centres**
- ✪ **Catalogues**
- ✪ **Mail order**
- ✪ **Websites**
- ✪ **Ticket machines**
- ✪ **Rail, road and air**

When deciding on a distribution channel, here are some aspects to consider:

- ✪ **The image of the product**
- ✪ **The size of the product**
- ✪ **The number or range of products on sale**
- ✪ **The amount of storage space needed**
- ✪ **The preference of the customers**
- ✪ **The competition**
- ✪ **The money available**
- ✪ **The staffing demands**
- ✪ **The reliability of the distribution method**

The chosen method needs to be appropriate for the product. It needs to provide the best and simplest way for the customer to buy the product, so it should be accessible and attractive. For example, it must be easy to obtain, order and pay for clothes bought from a catalogue selling high-quality clothes direct to the customer and distributed by post. The catalogue must also be attractive, showing off the clothes in a positive way that will maximise sales.

Consider two leisure and recreation venues, one on a national level and one on a local level. If you were buying a site to build these venues, name the ten most important aspects you would consider? Do you feel the site is the correct one for the particular venue? Give reasons for your answers and discuss them with your friends.

Consider two leisure and recreation products that are distributed to the customer in two different ways. If you can, choose one that is sold via the internet. Assess how attractive and accessible these methods are. Suppose you are in charge of sales for these products, what advice would you give to help improve their distribution?

Price

Pricing is a vital aspect of the marketing mix. Every product has a price. Price is the intermediary between the product and the customer. Every product has a price range in which customers will buy it. This is called price elasticity. Pricing decisions must fall within this range – not too high or too low. Even small price fluctuations can have a huge effect on demand and sales. Petrol prices are a good example. Some people will drive around their local garages to find a litre that costs a penny cheaper.

The purpose of pricing is to record a market valuation or the worth of a product. Generally we recognise that the best costs more, so we regard price as an indication of quality. However, most people do not buy the best; they buy the product that seems to be the best value for money. But the product must meet their requirements. There is a continual trade-off between price and quality. We must recognise the importance the customer places on price in order to maximise sales. Duracell batteries are a good example. They cost more than the other batteries but they last longer; customers are happy with this trade-off and perceive Duracell batteries as good value. Here are some aspects to consider:

- **Basic price**
- **Discounts (Table 4.9)**
- **Special promotions**
- **Methods of payment**
    cash
    cheque

credit card

debit card

interest-free credit

Price determination

When you are setting the price of a product, you will need to consider the objectives and policies of the organisation. Here are some factors that could influence your decision:

✪ **Profit and sales targets**

✪ **Cash recovery on investment already spent**

✪ **Market share targets**

✪ **Promotion and loss leading**

✪ **Price elasticity**

✪ **Competition**

Profit and sales targets should be over all timescales: short, medium and long. Cash recovery on investment means making sales to get back the money you've already spent.

Loss leading is where a product may be underpriced or subsidised in order to generate initial interest and sales. Once the product has become established, the price may then increase. This tactic is often employed when launching a new magazine. When you're devising a pricing policy – a statement specifying your prices and the reasons for them – you will need to consider all these aspects.

Table 4.9 *Admission rates for Warwick Castle in 1999: have a look at the concessions*

1 Mar to 31 May and 1 Sept to 29 Feb 2000	Groups (min 20)	Individuals	1 June to 31 Aug	Groups (min 20)	Individuals
Adults	£7.75	£9.50	Adults	£8.50	£10.50
Children (4–16 years)	£5.00	£5.80	Children (4–16 years)	£5.25	£6.25
Students	£6.70	£7.25	Students	£7.25	£7.80
Senior citizens	£6.15	£6.85	Senior citizens	£6.75	£7.50
Family ticket (2 adults + 2 children)	–	£27.00	Family ticket (2 adults + 2 children)	–	£28.00

Prices include full admission to castle, grounds and garden
Prices are per person and include VAT at 17.5%

The role of price

Pricing is often considered the most important aspect of the marketing mix because it has a big influence on the customer and because it is so easy to change. However, it is only part of the overall marketing strategy and should complement the other variables, e.g. pricing reductions for new products.

> Keep an eye on your competitors' prices and their pricing policies. You may lose custom if your prices are more expensive but your products are no different

Some groups of customers may receive price reductions. In the public sector these groups may pay concessionary rates so they can still afford to enjoy a particular service:

- ✪ **Unemployed people**
- ✪ **Children**
- ✪ **Students**
- ✪ **Pensioners**

Exercise 4.4

Consider a product or service in leisure and recreation, e.g. a swim. Identify something the same or similar but provided by another organisation, e.g. a swim at a local authority leisure centre and a swim at a leisure pool with water slides and flumes.

★ What is the price difference? Maybe it's almost zero.

★ Suggest some reasons for the difference.

★ Which service do you think provides value for money and why?

Promotion

Promotion is a method of communicating with customers; it looks at how an organisation can persuade a customer to buy a product for the first time then how to make that customer forever loyal to the product and the organisation. Promotion and advertising are often confused. There are many forms of promotion; advertising is just one of them.

Advertising

Advertising aims to persuade the customer to see a product or service in the way the advertiser wants. It can be characterised in four statements:

- ✪ **It is one-way**
- ✪ **It must be paid for**
- ✪ **It is a public announcement**
- ✪ **It is designed to influence the customer**

Direct marketing

Direct marketing involves direct communication with the customer to influence them in a certain way. Here are some examples:

- ✪ **Addressed letters or correspondence – a mailshot**
- ✪ **Unaddressed letters or correspondence – a maildrop**
- ✪ **Catalogues detailing products and services on offer**
- ✪ **Flyers delivered to the door of the customer**
- ✪ **Telemarketing**
- ✪ **Internet marketing**

Public relations

News coverage, radio interviews, etc., are sought through public relations promotions, often involving press releases. If the media consider a press release newsworthy – worth covering – they may use it without charging you. If this strategy is unsuccessful, you may have to pay for wider advertising. Sometimes public relations agencies perform these tasks. Here are some other tasks they might perform.

- ✪ **Product launches**
- ✪ **Parties for new and existing customers.**
    They celebrate a product
    They stimulate sales

- ✪ **Performing the media interviews on behalf of an organisation**
- ✪ **Producing an image to help promote a product or service**

Public relations agencies are becoming more popular. It can be argued that initial success is down to the professionalism of the product launch. If the launch and promotions are poorly planned and managed, the product could flop or it may need a relaunch. See the product life cycle on page 157.

Personal selling

Covered in more detail in Unit 5, personal selling is the promotion of a product by a person. Here the salesperson has a huge influence on the success of a product or service. Important characteristics in a salesperson include:

- ✪ **Suitable personality for the role**
- ✪ **Product knowledge**
- ✪ **Organisational knowledge**
- ✪ **Knowledge of the industry and competitors**
- ✪ **The ability to communicate and negotiate**
- ✪ **Appropriate appearance**

Sales promotion

Sales promotion covers a range of activities. A common way is to have an occasional advertising campaign to stimulate sales. The aim is to persuade the customer to go and buy something, or at least to consider a purchase in the future. This sort of campaign adds a sense of urgency to the overall promotion. Sales promotions are often short and sharp; they need to be memorable. Here are some examples:

- ✪ **Introductory offers**
- ✪ **Trial offers**
- ✪ **Two for the price of one**
- ✪ **Money-off coupons**
- ✪ **Free services**
- ✪ **Competitions**

Sponsorship

Sponsorship creates a link or association between a product or service and another product, service, person or organisation. The aim is to jointly promote a service linking two audiences or groups of customers. Many football clubs are sponsored by organisations, and the sponsor's name appears on the football kit. The sponsor hopes that viewers of football will become more aware of their products and services, and they hope it will increase sales.

Packaging

Packaging is promotion through design and display. The way a product looks to the customer can influence whether or not they buy it. Activities and adverts aimed at children are often brightly coloured and have popular characters. Without these colours and characters, would children choose the products?

Summary

An organisation needs to use a selection of promotional methods that will maximise public awareness and so increase sales. Here are five aspects to consider:

✪ *The product itself*: **The higher the price, the more persuading people take. The promotion for one swim is likely to be more modest than the promotion for a £1500 membership to a private gym. The higher the price, the more personal the selling. People want to negotiate and discuss what they are getting for their money**

✪ *The target customers*: **Advertising appears to be much more influential in the service industries and where industries sell their products and services to the public instead of other organisations. Leisure and recreation is a service industry that is customer focused**

✪ *The product life cycle*: **The depth and strength of a promotion will depend on the product's stage in its life cycle. A product on the point of being launched needs to create maximum awareness to stimulate interest and sales; this requires a comprehensive promotional effort. Classic products with consistent sales over several years will need less promotional effort**

✪ *Available money*: **The money in the promotions budget will influence the activities that are planned**

✪ *Technology*: **The late 1990s have seen the growth of the internet. This provides a valuable method of communications with the customer. It is possible to search on the internet and connect with a website. For example, if you were looking to start a new fitness plan and wanted to employ a fitness instructor, you could enter 'fitness' into a search engine and it would come up with a list of websites having some connection**

to fitness. The opportunities are endless. Don't forget the internet if you want to remain competitive

Activity 4.2

In a group of four, choose one product or service from the leisure and recreation industry that you all know well. If you want to, think of yourselves as the customers, your school or college as the promoter, and your Vocational A-level as the product. But choose something else if you prefer. Each of you on your own should look at all these aspects of the product or service:

★ Advertising

★ Direct marketing

★ Public relations

★ Personal selling

★ Sales promotions

★ Sponsorship

Now get together again, answer these questions then produce a joint summary that explains your conclusions in no more than 200 words.

★ Do you all remember the same parts?

★ Did the same promotional aspects influence you to buy or use the product or service?

★ What can you conclude about the promotional activities of the product or service?

Conclusion

All variables affect each other. It is little use improving the promotion of a product without considering the influence of price, place and the product itself. The variables within the marketing mix will be considered in detail and used as part of the overall marketing plan.

Market research

Market research aims to gather accurate information on customer needs. It links to the first stage of the marketing process, where customers are classified and their needs identified.

The more information we gather, the better the outcome will be. Having more information allows us to meet the demands of the customer more closely. However, the information that we gather must be useful and relevant. We may want to know lots of different bits of information. Here are some possible areas:

✪ **The internal and external customer**

What do they want?

Where do they want it?

✪ **The product**

Does it meet the needs of the customer?

Is it attractive to the customer?

✪ **Sales**

Do the sales levels meet the targets of the organisation?

✪ **Promotions**

Do these promotions help trigger sales or not?

✪ **National economics**

Is the country in recession?

Will recession affect leisure and recreation?

✪ **Competition in terms of:**

quality

price

range

Having decided what information to collect, the next thing is to decide how to collect it. There are two methods of gathering information: field research and desk research. Field research is also called primary research; desk research is also called secondary research.

Field research

Field research means going into the field and gathering information for yourself. In geography the field may be a swamp or a mudflat, but in marketing it's the marketplace. Here are some examples of field research:

Did You Know?

○ McDonald's questionnaires are small and bright with smiley faces
○ BT phones its customers to get feedback and sell new services

○ **Questionnaires**
○ **Personal experience**
○ **Surveys**
○ **Observations**
○ **Physical evidence (for sports science)**
○ **Focus groups**
○ **Suggestion schemes**
○ **Mystery shoppers**

This information can be gathered in several ways:

○ **By post**
○ **By telephone**
○ **Face-to-face**
○ **On the internet**

Internet research is becoming more and more popular. Successful field research, particularly written research, should have these characteristics:

○ **Clear and precise**
○ **Well structured**
○ **Includes instructions**
○ **Information gathered in a logical order**
○ **Questions gather all aspects of desired information**
○ **No double questions**
○ **Grammatically sound**
○ **Simple language**
○ **Attractive**
○ **Sponsored to add credibility**
○ **Easy to code and analyse**
○ **Easy to complete**
○ **Encourages maximum response**
○ **Encourages minimum error**
○ **Gathers names and addresses for a mailing list**

Field research needs to gather a representative sample of customers' views. To do this you need to consider sampling. There are two main types of sampling, random and non-random:

✪ *Random research* **ensures each person has an equal chance of being selected to provide information**

✪ *Non-random research* **is where individuals or groups of individuals are selected to provide information**

Choosing an appropriate method can help to minimise error and ensure the accuracy of the gathered information. Other errors can occur when:

✪ **The information is gathered in an inappropriate fashion**

> Asking questions customers cannot understand
>
> Omitting to ask the important questions

✪ **The methods chosen are not comprehensive**

✪ **The customers providing the information are not representative**

✪ **The interviewer influences the answers of the customer**

✪ **The customer gives answers to please the interviewer**

> A customer is asked whether they smoke
>
> The customer believes that smoking will be frowned on
>
> The customer claims not to smoke
>
> The customer actually smokes 10 cigarettes a day

✪ **The information is inaccurately scored**

Here are some advantages of field research:

✪ **The information you gather will be up to date**

✪ **The method of gathering the information is flexible**

✪ **You can choose to complete a survey or talk to customers**

✪ **You should feel confident in your conclusions**

✪ **You should know your conclusions to be accurate**

Here are some disadvantages of field research:

✪ **It can be expensive and time-consuming during:**

> planning and preparation
>
> data gathering
>
> analysis and completion

✪ **It can take a long time to gather information that might be needed quickly**

✪ **It can be open to error**

✪ **It may be difficult to find out the information you want**

The best way to ensure the accuracy and usefulness of your information is to minimise errors and to gather it in several different ways.

Desk research

Desk research means gathering information while sitting at your desk – there's no need to go into the field. Perhaps the information has already been collected and published. There are two types of desk research, internal and external.

- ✪ *Internal research* **uses information that the organisation may already have collected; this includes:**

    sales records

    customer comments

    analysis of competitors

    databases

    visitor numbers

- ✪ *External research* **is information that is published from outside the organisation; this includes:**

    government and international statistics

    industry reports

    company reports

    books

    magazines

Here are some advantages of desk research:

- ✪ **Cheap – no effort to gather information**
- ✪ **Quick – the information is already there**
- ✪ **Easy to use**
- ✪ **Can provide useful support to primary research**

Here are some disadvantages of desk research:

- ✪ **The information gathered may not be exactly what you need**
- ✪ **It could be out of date**
- ✪ **You could misinterpret the information**
- ✪ **The information may not be accessible**
- ✪ **The information may not have been gathered yet**

When you're gathering your data, you need to use both field research and desk research to provide the whole picture of what the customer wants. You also need to minimise any errors. The more relevant the information you gather, the better your chance of success.

After you've done your market research, you need to analyse it and put your findings into action. Make the best possible decisions to maximise your sales. If you don't analyse and act on your data, there's no point in collecting it.

Activity 4.3

The manager of a local nightclub, located on an out-of-town retail park, has asked you to carry out some market research. She is hoping to expand and open a nightclub in a neighbouring city in a similar location but this city has some well-known nightclubs based in the centre. Produce an action plan of how you would gather this information, justifying your decisions.

Marketing communications

Now we have looked at researching our customer needs, the next stage is to tell the customers our message in a way that persuades them to buy our product or service. This is called marketing communications.

In addition to these we will look at advertising and sponsorship.

When you are looking at marketing communications you need to consider all these parts of the chapter and Unit 5 Customer Services too.

Advertising

▼ ▼ ▼ ▼ ▼ ▼ ▼ ▼ ▼

Advertising
a paid form of non-personal communication that aims to influence the customer in a particular way

▲ ▲ ▲ ▲ ▲ ▲ ▲ ▲ ▲

Advertising is part of an overall promotions plan and part of the marketing mix. It is a powerful method of communicating with the customer. Think of how many adverts you can immediately identify.

Advertising is a persuasive form of communication; the advertiser is aiming to convince the customer about the qualities of its products or services. It uses advertising to make the customer see its products in the way it wants. Earlier on we described advertising as:

- ✪ **one-way**
- ✪ **paid**
- ✪ **a public announcement**
- ✪ **designed to influence the customer**

Advertising is based on a number of assumptions:

- ✪ **Not every customer knows what they want or need**
- ✪ **Not every customer knows which product or service meets these needs**
- ✪ **Customer satisfaction is not forever**
- ✪ **All advertising wants customers to become loyal forever**

Characteristics of successful advertising include:

- ✪ **Distinctive and memorable**
- ✪ **Attractive to the target audience**
- ✪ **Uses appropriate language, avoiding jargon**

Table 4.10 *Methods of advertising: advantages and disadvantages*

Method of advertising	Advantages	Disadvantages
Press	Reaches a large audience, especially free newspapers Local, regional or national Cost varies from £30 to £5000	Some people don't read papers People may miss the advert Some people may need to be reached in another language
Television	Creates massive awareness Simple and dynamic Regarded highly by the public Uses sound as well as vision	Not for local campaigns Very expensive
Radio	Reaches blind people Reaches older people Can be very targeted	Can be expensive
Magazines	Visually attractive Can be very targeted	Can be expensive
Internet	Attracts many customers Purchases are easy Proactive way to advertise Websites are cheap to set up Uses sight and sound E-commerce is in fashion	Not everyone has access Maintaining a website needs some technical knowledge Keywords (meta tags) are crucial to maximise site hits
Leaflets	Costs are usually low Small effort, big awareness Can be very targeted Customers can keep them	Can be messy Can seem a bit dated

✪ **Enhances the image of the organisation, product or service**

✪ **Has good timing, e.g. tennis gear during Wimbledon**

Advertising can consist of one advert or a series of adverts, usually known as a campaign. For advertising to be successful, you need to repeat things to the customer, so campaigns are often planned to run over a period and using different methods to get the message across. This should attract as many customers as possible. Table 4.10 lists some advertising methods.

For an advertising campaign to be successful, it needs to be part of an overall plan. Before starting out, you should consider:

✪ **The specific product**

✪ **The image and type of campaign**

✪ **What you want the customer to think**

✪ **The timing**

✪ **The amount of money available**

✪ **Tactics**

✪ **The target market**

The law affects all marketing communications, and advertising in particular. Here are some laws to be aware of.

Trade Descriptions Act 1968

The Trade Descriptions Act aims to prevent false or misleading statements being made about products or services.

Consumer Protection Act 1987

The Consumer Protection Act is divided into three areas:

✪ *Product liability*: **this aims to protect the customer from defective products, either by design or manufacture**

✪ *Consumer safety*: **this aims to protect the customer from buying goods or services that are unsafe**

✪ *Misleading pricing*: **it is unlawful to give the customer an indication of a price which is misleading**

Data Protection Act 1998

The Data Protection Act ensures that personal data can only be:

✪ **Obtained lawfully**

✪ **Used for its original purpose**

- ✪ **Accurate and up to date**
- ✪ **Kept securely**

Regulatory bodies

Regulatory bodies also control and influence the standard of advertising we see. They ensure that adverts are accurate, do not offend anyone and are acceptable to the customers. Advertising is powerful but it needs to be planned and considered in order to be a success.

Activity 4.4

- ★ Think of your favourite sporting activity. Produce an advert to convince a newcomer to give it a go.

- ★ Video a series of adverts from the television. Choose different times, perhaps just before the evening news, early in the morning, later during the day. Assess who the adverts are aimed at and what message they try to put across. Do they do it successfully?

- ★ Investigate the price of advertising on your local commercial radio station. Do you consider it to be value for money?

Sponsorship

Over the past 20 or 30 years, the leisure and recreation industry, particularly sport, has become much more popular as a method of marketing communications. It helps create an awareness of an organisation or a product by connecting it to a sporting team or star. It has also introduced large sums of money into sport. Sometimes this money has gone to individuals and sometimes into the sport itself.

Main advantages

- ✪ **It creates massive exposure in many other forms**
- ✪ **It is novel and creative**
- ✪ **It is not as cluttered as television and newspapers**
- ✪ **Customers convert sporting loyalty into product loyalty**
- ✪ **It's persistent and hard to turn off**

Other advantages

✪ The communication takes a soft-sell approach; it is subtle. The customer is getting bored with the aggressive hard sell and this provides a refreshing contrast

✪ Sport can create a symbolic image; sport is seen as healthy, positive and beneficial

✪ It can be used to counteract a negative image, so it is sought by organisations that sell alcohol, cigarettes, etc.

✪ It is cheap compared with some other methods

✪ Sport is seen more and more as a place to do business. Football stadiums attract corporate clients who aim to please and persuade their clients to do deals while they enjoy a football match. Sponsorship can provide this avenue and impress these clients

✪ Sport is often targeted to certain customer types; this can be useful if you need to adopt market segmentation as part of your overall marketing strategy

✪ Awareness can be created on a local, regional, national or international level depending on the team or the individual

Some disadvantages

✪ Bad publicity of a sporting team or star can have disastrous repercussions for an organisation

✪ You need to select the correct star as a method of communication; there is little room for error. If you want to create a bad boy image, use a footballer that has a bad boy image, not someone squeaky clean

✪ It is difficult to quantify the success of marketing communications through sponsorship; it is also difficult to control

✪ A product could suffer overexposure. Perhaps the customers do not notice an important logo or name, it just seems to merge with the star or the team

✪ Sponsorship can be damaging to the sport itself. The money it attracts can induce some athletes to cheat, perhaps by drug taking

✪ There have also been concerns that sponsorship can exert an unhealthy influence. Events may be managed to please the sponsors. Allegations include cricketers bowling towards an advertising board, sponsored footballers playing when not properly fit, and sponsored athletes retiring before they are ready

Control it

Sponsorship offers great opportunities but it does need to be controlled. A lack of proper control could undermine competitiveness and threaten the very meaning of sport.

Activity 4.5

See if you can identify the sponsors of the following sporting stars, teams and events:

★ Manchester United Football Club

★ Tim Henman

★ Basketball League

★ Rugby

★ Snooker

★ Formula One

Now see if you can identify the sporting stars, teams or events linked to these organisations:

★ Carling

★ Nike

★ Adidas

★ Renault Laguna

★ Cadbury

Using local newspapers identify sports sponsorship on a local level; consider:

★ The benefits to the sponsors

★ The benefits to the individual or team

★ Assess their value

If you look back at the unit objectives, you will see that we have successfully covered all five of them. You should now have a detailed understanding of the marketing unit for the Vocational A-level in Leisure and Recreation. The final stage is to put it into action.

Marketing in action

The levels and standards of marketing in the leisure and recreation industry vary dramatically depending on the sector of leisure and recreation and the organisation itself. However, there are some common guidelines that can be easily adopted by all leisure and recreation providers. By following these guidelines it is possible to produce a useful marketing plan and strategy.

A marketing plan and strategy look at all the relevant aspects and variables of marketing and put them into some sort of order. This plan documents how the marketing objectives will be met. The methods used are the marketing strategies.

Each organisation has a unique set of resources, ranging from the buildings and equipment to the people that work within. A marketing plan will take into account all these resources. It will also take into account the strengths and weaknesses of the organisation, aiming to maximise the strengths and minimise the weaknesses. The marketing plan provides direction as it helps plan for the future. Here are some of the benefits:

- ✪ **Allows planning over all timescales**
    - short
    - medium
    - long
- ✪ **Helps plan for change**
- ✪ **Improves communication and motivation**
- ✪ **Forces a detailed look at all operations**
- ✪ **Makes the most of the resources available**
- ✪ **Helps the organisation remain competitive**

Producing a marketing plan

A marketing plan should be split into three areas: a historical review, a situational analysis, the future plan or marketing strategy. Situational analysis is a major part of the marketing plan. It provides a snapshot of the organisation at one particular moment, almost as if you could take a photograph and use it to describe the marketing variables. The future plan or strategy studies the situational analysis in detail, looking at each aspect and putting together suggestions for future improvements.

A historical review should include

- ✪ **When the organisation was established**
- ✪ **Ownership of the organisation**
- ✪ **Sector of the organisation**
- ✪ **What it produced originally and how this has changed**
- ✪ **Any notable events and the reasons for them**
  - successes
  - failures
  - changes

A situational analysis should include

- ✪ **Marketing objectives**
- ✪ **Internal and external factors influencing marketing**
- ✪ **Annual turnover**
- ✪ **Sales figures and targets**
- ✪ **Sales and selling techniques**
- ✪ **Target markets and customers**
- ✪ **Product**
- ✪ **Place**
- ✪ **Price**
- ✪ **Promotion**
- ✪ **Advertising**
- ✪ **Sponsorship**
- ✪ **Competition**
- ✪ **Programming**
- ✪ **Market research and industry trends**
- ✪ **Numbers of staff employed**
- ✪ **Organisational structures**
- ✪ **Diversification**

A future plan should include

- ✪ **Aims and objectives for all timescales**
- ✪ **New and creative ideas**
- ✪ **Recommendations**

Now we will look at two case studies. Case studies are the best way to practise putting a marketing plan into action. The Phoenix case study looks at the marketing of a sports team and how to change its fortunes. The Arctic case study considers how to market a new sports product. Marketing plans are not one-off analyses; they should be carried out on an annual basis.

Phoenix Suns

Using the information below, conduct a SWOT analysis and prepare a future marketing plan to improve the performance of the Phoenix Suns basketball team.

▶ HISTORICAL REVIEW

The Phoenix Suns are an American basketball team established in 1968 as a franchise to the city of Phoenix in Arizona. There were many original owners, most of them wealthy and famous

The aim of the Phoenix Suns was to produce a recognised and worthy reputation

Immediately work began on an ambitious and comprehensive building programme; this was constantly changed to keep up with the times

There were also constant changes to the team, players and the management of the club

During the first season their scores were disappointing but during the next two seasons they improved. The reason for this was the further extension of a sports development plan

By the fifth season the picture had changed and there was a drastic drop in league positions and scores

A change in strategy was needed to improve the motivation of everyone in the team

continued

continued

▶ SITUATIONAL ANALYSIS

This highlighted five problem areas:

- ★ Injury and illness of leading players
- ★ Lack of players available in the development team
- ★ Poor motivation and commitment
- ★ Insufficient talent
- ★ A drop in performance

    poor performance meant low attendance

    low attendance meant lower profits

And here are some other points to consider:

- ★ The team is situated in a large metropolitan area with vast expanding suburbs
- ★ Spectators are mostly professionals and non-working women
- ★ Phoenix is multicultural with many established allegiances to other sporting teams
- ★ The weather is warm and dry and there are already many other popular and varied sport and recreational activities such as hockey, athletics and baseball
- ★ Over 30% of spectators are season ticket holders and over 500 of these are corporate clients
- ★ 27% of spectators had their ticket given to them
- ★ 23% attended once or twice
- ★ 22% attended all games
- ★ 35% would attend if the price of the tickets were reduced
- ★ 33% would attend more if the performance of the team improved
- ★ Promotional activities were on two levels:

continued

continued

> TV, radio, newspapers and direct mail promoted season tickets
>
> Posters, direct mail, themed nights and giveaway games promoted individual tickets

▶ MARKETING PLAN

Put together a plan which copes with:

- ★ A fall in attendance
- ★ A disappointing season
- ★ Increased competition

Here are some aspects to consider:

- ★ Customer profile
- ★ Competition
- ★ Promotion
- ★ Programming
- ★ Pricing
- ★ Selling
- ★ Distribution
- ★ Image

Perhaps compare and contrast the Phoenix Suns with a sporting team you know well.

Arctic

► HISTORICAL REVIEW

In 1987, Arctic were faced with the need to develop a marketing strategy for a new product, the Wetbike, which was to be put on general sale the following year

Arctic also produce a snowmobile; this has reached saturation in the product life cycle, so Arctic feel it is now time to diversify

The Wetbike aims to make Arctic a year-round success

Arctic are financially sound and they've had proven success in other areas

► SITUATIONAL ANALYSIS

Here are some of the Wetbike's features:

★ Powered by a 50 horsepower jet pump
★ Can reach speeds of 48 kph
★ Easy to ride and not too noisy
★ Instruction takes just one hour
★ Pulls a waterskier on top of the water
★ Has an exclusivity licence
★ Efficient on fuel
★ Carries two passengers
★ Looks like a luxury

The product is aimed at:

★ Customers with a high disposable income
★ The young and middle-aged

There are three similar brands and one of them has the main market share. Previous market research by Arctic has suggested there is room for two leading brands. Besides that, Arctic believe their product has several advantages:

continued

continued

★ More powerful

★ Safer as there is no propeller

★ Carries an extra passenger
   (2 instead of 1)

★ Greater performance and economy

★ Greater passenger comfort

▶ MARKETING PLAN

You now need to put together a future marketing plan to launch the Wetbike. Also, consider the following headings and conduct a PEST analysis:

★ Promotion to create the initial awareness
   videos
   demos
   sponsors

★ Distribution

★ Pricing, including credit terms and customer profiles

★ Further diversification such as a children's Wetbike

★ The product life cycle

Do you think the Wetbike will be a success?

Revision questions

1 Define marketing.

2 Name three internal factors that can affect marketing.

3 Name three external factors that can affect marketing.

4 List five characteristics of a successful marketing objective.

5 Identify four methods of gathering information from the customer.

6 List three ways of classifying the customer.

7 State the four P's of the marketing mix.

8 Identify three methods of distribution.

9 What do you understand by price elasticity?

10 Identify three groups that may enjoy concessionary pricing.

11 Describe the characteristics of successful personal selling.

12 Why is sports sponsorship so attractive to sport and to organisations wanting to sponsor it?

13 Use the product life cycle to describe a flop, a gimmick and a classic.

14 List five examples of primary research.

15 What is another name for secondary research?

16 List five examples of secondary research.

17 State four methods of advertising.

18 What are the three stages of a marketing plan?

Filling a Gap in the Market

BACKGROUND

Ever since you can remember, you have wanted to be a success in business. You admire Richard Branson. You are aiming to be someone. You also think you have come up with a gap in the market – your way to reach your dream. But from your vocational studies, you know you need an idea that works. There is no room for error. You are going to produce an extensive marketing plan that will keep you focused on your dream.

TASKS

★ Identify your marketing objectives, making sure they are clear, realistic and measurable

★ Produce a historical review – analyse products or services similar to yours and do some research on your competitors

★ Identify and evaluate all factors that could affect the success of your idea

★ Prepare a future plan – the route to your success:

be original and be specific

look at all timescales

Customer service

Objectives

- **Be able to describe and understand customer service**
- **Demonstrate the importance of excellent customer service**
- **Identify the importance of personal presentation**
- **Identify types of customer**
- **Investigate sales and selling techniques**
- **Demonstrate the ability to deal with customers successfully**
- **Demonstrate the ability to handle complaints and comments**
- **Measure customer service**
- **Apply all these areas to the leisure and recreation industry**

Customer service
ensuring the customer receives what they expect to receive

Successful customer service
ensuring the customer receives what they expect, plus a little bit more

Customer service has close links to marketing (Unit 4) and also the optional unit on human resources. To get the full picture, read this unit alongside Units 4 and 6.

Customer service is about people and how they behave. It is about meeting the customer's expectations and desires. It is about being fair and courteous and treating people with respect. **Successful customer service** is difficult and complex. Customer service covers many areas, including the initial awareness of a service or product, handing over money, and what happens when things go wrong.

It can be argued that customer service is relatively easy to understand, it is after all full of common sense. People like to be addressed in a pleasant manner and in a way they can understand. However, it is not so easy to put into practice, particularly when it involves a critical look at ourselves. Try to understand the purpose of customer service before you put it into practice.

Some background

The term 'customer service' seems to be associated with America and particularly phrases like 'Have a nice day' and 'You're welcome'. It is commonly thought that customer service originated in America, and it is true that America prides itself on being the market leader in customer service. In the UK we have largely followed this lead, and the 1990s have seen a boom in customer service.

During the 1990s the government introduced the Citizen's Charter; this stated what everyone could expect from public services. It also introduced the Patient's Charter to cover customer service in the NHS. Regulators were created to keep tabs on newly privatised utilities, e.g. Ofwat for water and Oftel for telecoms.

On television there was a rise in the number of consumer programmes. The BBC's 'Watchdog' went out in the early evening, catching a prime time audience. The leisure and recreation industry has its own customer service standards; for example, the AA and the RAC both grade hotels and tourist attractions. Customers now seem more aware of what they should receive and more ready to complain when they don't receive it.

The private sector has traditionally been more customer focused. This is simply because if you please a customer they return and tell their friends; this increases sales and leads to greater profit. The major aim of the private sector is to make money, and successful customer service is one way to achieve it. Through government initiatives, such as the Citizen's Charter, the public sector must also consider its customer service.

Customer service is a challenge. All customers are different and we all have our own needs, so it is impossible to please everyone. Perfection is hard to achieve. Sometimes we cannot fulfil the needs of the customer; later in this unit we will see how to handle these situations.

> Customer service is not always saying what the customer wants to hear

Why service matters

Customer service is an essential part of any industry. Without customers there would be no business. To understand customer service in the leisure and recreation industry, we must take a look at the things it sells.

A product or a good is something tangible that can be seen and touched, e.g. a tennis racket or a pair of trainers. A service is intangible; it happens once and then it is over. You cannot try on a service before you buy it. Examples are a game of squash, a football match and a roller coaster ride.

The leisure and recreation industry sells products and services, but it is mainly considered a service industry. Because it is impossible to try on or watch a service before it is bought, the actual sale can be greatly influenced by people, past experiences and recommendations. All these influences are part of customer service, and service industries make great efforts to please their customers. They want them to have good memories, to come back again and to tell other people.

Bad news is always attractive. If you think about your everyday life, you do tend to remember the bad experiences more vividly than the good ones. This is true of customer service; we tend to talk about what went wrong more than what went right. We talk in detail about what went wrong, but things that went right were 'just great'. Think about your first night out with a new date. You have a brilliant night, lots of laughs, a follow-up date but the part you remember most is where you spilled your drink all over your date's new clothes. The bad bits come back all too clearly.

In customer service it is essential that the 'bad bits' are kept to a minimum, but it's impossible to prevent them altogether. When they do happen, try to keep them as quiet as possible. The fewer the customers who find out, the better it is.

If we meet the needs of the customer, the customer does tend to return, perhaps many times. Again it is basic human nature to want security. If we feel secure about what we do, we don't tend to change it. Human beings appear to be creatures of habit. It is useful to categorise customers in terms of their loyalty:

✪ **Some customers go to the same place and never go elsewhere; they're loyal forever**
✪ **Some customers are on the whole loyal to one place but do try elsewhere very occasionally**
✪ **Some customers have a favourite place but chop and change on a regular basis**
✪ **Some customers go wherever it's convenient and have no pattern**

THE EFFECTS OF SUCCESSFUL CUSTOMER SERVICE

HAPPY CUSTOMER

They tell their friends about it

↓

ENHANCED
IMAGE

The happy customer returns to spend more money

↓

The happy customer's friends also go and spend their money

↓

Now both are LOYAL FOREVER!

↓

Increase in sales

↓

Increase in profits

↓

Sometimes this means more pay, better working conditions

↓

Secure jobs – happy staff

↓

Even better customer service

Happy customers return and spend more money

Most organisations will want their customers to be loyal forever. The aim is to convert the other three types. If a customer visits your leisure centre out of curiosity, try to make them so impressed they will return forever. They will never again visit another leisure centre in the local area. Some customers shop in the same food hall every week; they don't look at the price of the food they buy, they are happy with the service as a whole. Companies encourage this type of custom by providing loyalty cards that give discounts. The more money people spend, the greater the discount they get. Lifelong loyalty leads to larger sales and bigger profits. Here are some hints:

✪ **The effects of successful customer service should be communicated to all; it should be clear to everyone what the benefits are**

✪ **It is human nature to want to please. Successful customer service can help to increase job satisfaction, reduce complaints and make work a pleasure instead of a chore**

✪ **Customer service is beneficial to everyone**

THE UNHAPPY CUSTOMER

They tell their friends
about it

↓

POOR
REPUTATION

The unhappy customer wants a refund or does NOT return
↓
The unhappy customer's friends do not spend their money here either
↓
Decrease in sales
Even a loss
↓
No £'s
↓
Poor working conditions
No money for pay rises
Unhappy staff
Insecure jobs
↓
Even worse customer care
↓
BANKRUPTCY

Exercise 5.1

Customer care is quite a recent phenomenon in the UK. You
have applied for a job as an assistant manager in a local
leisure centre and have been invited for interview. As part of
the selection process you have got to produce a presentation
entitled 'Is customer care worth the bother?' You firmly
believe it is. How do you persuade the interview panel?
What would you include?

Now we understand a bit more about customer service – why it's important to organisations and how it fits into leisure and recreation – let's take a closer look at the customer.

Personal presentation

People play an important part in the leisure and recreation industry. They can be the difference between success and failure. It is possible to tell a lot about a person from the way they look and the way they present themselves. Sometimes these assumptions are accurate, but not always. All organisations aim to present a professional image and all members of staff should try to do the same.

First impressions are exceptionally important because they tend to last. The customer can also make assumptions from this first impression, e.g. 'He looks miserable, can't be much fun here. I'll try somewhere else.' In leisure and recreation, first impressions must be good impressions. For example, a member of staff who has regular contact with the public should always be smart, clean, professional and appropriately dressed. Suitable dress may not be a traditional suit; it's whatever is usually worn in that particular role. A smart tracksuit is more appropriate for a lifeguard. Taking this a step further, a sports coach needn't be nearly 2 m tall with a six-pack stomach and designer clothes. As long as they can inspire confidence, their looks are not important.

Appropriate dress and personal hygiene

Wear the right clothes

- ✪ *Functional*: **appropriate for the job**
- ✪ *Clean*: **coffee stains don't look attractive**
- ✪ *Smart*: **creased shirts look unprofessional**
- ✪ *Discreet*: **a leotard is fine in the gym but not on reception**

Have clean hair and fresh breath

- ✪ **Look generally clean and tidy**
- ✪ **Have hair that is clean and neat**
- ✪ **Make sure your breath is fresh**

Remember the simple things

Dress and personal hygiene do need to be tackled. It's amazing how simple things can affect our choice. Perhaps a customer is put off a swimming instructor because they smell of stale cigarettes. Perhaps a room retains some body odour even after cleaning and people are discouraged.

Personal attitude

Each member of staff is a paid representative of the organisation and should always act in a professional manner to create the best possible impression. Here are some dos and don'ts.

Dos

✪ **Be loyal to the organisation**

✪ **Follow organisational procedures**

✪ **Respect the buildings and equipment where you work**

✪ **Be friendly and courteous with colleagues and customers**

✪ **Separate private and professional life as far as possible**

✪ **Respect the views of others**

✪ **Treat colleagues and customers as you'd like to be treated yourself**

✪ **Be honest and constructive**

✪ **Ask if unsure**

Don'ts

✪ **Criticise the organisation in front of customers**

✪ **Discuss confidential details**

✪ **Argue or swear in front of customers**

✪ **Lose your temper at work**

✪ **Consume alcohol or smoke at work**

✪ **Act in a way that can put anyone at risk**

First impressions can be created when we talk to people, but often we make assumptions and create our own perceptions before a word has been spoken. When people play a big part in the success of an organisation, they must give out non-verbal messages in line with its aims. Newtown Leisure Centre wants to be seen as the market leader in the Midlands; it considers its customer service and facilities are second to none. The staff at Newtown Leisure Centre must be smart, knowledgeable and friendly. They would give a conflicting message if they were uninformed, unkempt and unkind.

'I've heard enough'
or 'I want to speak'

interested evaluation

boredom

negative, lie or
doubt

evaluation or decision
making

caution, negative

hard & fast
attitude, stubborn

honesty, openness

stalling, security

Not all communication is through words

The **non-verbal communication** must portray the aims of the organisation; the members of staff put these aims into action. All organisations will have certain expectations of an employee and the customer service they should provide. Successful employees will meet these expectations and sometimes they will better them.

Presenting the organisation

Presentation of staff is very important but so is presentation of the environment. If people need to be warm and friendly, then the environment should be equally welcoming. The environment means any buildings, equipment and surrounding areas. Have you ever been put off visiting a leisure centre because it didn't look very nice? Or have you ever driven up to a hotel apprehensive about what it will be like? Here are some aspects to consider:

- ✪ **There should be no health and safety risks to the customer. Swimming pool water should be properly balanced and not cause any skin irritation**

- ✪ **Security can include personal security and security of valuables. Lockers should be provided in changing areas and perhaps sufficient lighting in dark areas inside and outside a building**

- ✪ **Environments should have a comfortable temperature, neither too hot nor too cold. If a changing area is used by small children, it needs to be warm enough for them to change without shivering. In retail outlets the shoppers are often clothed for the outside temperature; make them welcoming not stifling. Temperature is often used as a marketing tool, e.g. fitness suites often advertise air conditioning in the summer**

- ✪ **Adequate lighting allows customers to see clearly**

- ✪ **Environments should be pleasing to the eye; often a customer will venture into a shop or centre because it looks nice. This may be because it was well signposted, it has pretty flower beds or there are attractive window displays. Any surrounding areas should look inviting**

Activity 5.1

Visit two leisure and recreation venues. While participating in an activity note your first impressions of a member of staff. Consider their attitude and appearance and what you would do to be a better member of staff. Be relevant and constructive.

Now consider the presentation of the venues you have chosen, concentrating on the buildings and equipment. Make three lists headed strengths, weaknesses and recommendations. Highlight the top five points that impressed you and the bottom five that put you off. Compare your notes with others in your class who may have visited the same or other venues.

By concentrating on some of these aspects it is possible to turn some non-users into regular users and then into loyal users. Presentation is vitally important because it is human nature to make assumptions on what we see, hear and feel. These assumptions can be greatly influenced by the presentation of people and environments.

Types of customer

We are all original, we are all different. No two people are exactly the same. What each individual chooses to do in their leisure time is right for them. There are no hard and fast rules; there are no right or wrong choices. In order to provide successful customer service, all customers need to be treated in a way that makes them feel special and, at the very least, meets their expectations. It is incredibly difficult to know what each person wants or expects and it is impossible to get this right all the time. We can only make an educated guess.

Before we look at how to deal with customers, let's try to classify them. We can divide them into two types, internal and external. This is not an exact classification; use it only as a guide. The same person may be an internal customer in one situation and an external customer in another situation. It may also depend on who they are with or what their expectations are. All will become clear.

Internal customers

▼ ▼ ▼ ▼ ▼ ▼ ▼ ▼ ▼

Internal customer
a customer who has a direct working relationship with the organisation, most commonly a member of staff

▲ ▲ ▲ ▲ ▲ ▲ ▲ ▲ ▲

Successful customer service starts at home. Any employee is an **internal customer** of the organisation that employs them. The internal customer has expectations that need to be met for them to be satisfied at work. For example, an employee expects to be paid at a certain rate, at a certain time and in a certain way.

Most employees know their worth and the value of the job they do. Most people have reasonable expectations and these expectations should be met. Most organisations want to treat their employees fairly, helping them to progress and feel valued. Here are some things an employee can expect from their employer:

✪ **Pay should be:**
    above the minimum wage
    on a specified date
    by a specified method

WHO IS THE CUSTOMER?

Everyone is a customer at some time

- ❂ **An itemised payslip**
- ❂ **An employment contract**
- ❂ **A safe environment to work in**
- ❂ **Fair and equal treatment**
- ❂ **Scheduled breaks**
- ❂ **A reasonable workload**
- ❂ **Clear guidelines**
- ❂ **Training and development**
- ❂ **Appropriate wash, rest and feeding facilities**
- ❂ **A staff handbook**

The employer has to be fair but so does the employee. Although the world may not be ideal, there are still basic rights that everyone should enjoy.

Activity 5.2

Consider a locality within a 32 km radius. On a map identify:

- ★ A family pub with soft play areas
- ★ A leisure centre with a swimming club
- ★ A private health facility
- ★ A sports stadium

If you can, choose a job for each of the four venues and find out how the rates of pay and working conditions differ. At which of them would you like to work and why?

Internal customer satisfaction is about what makes people happy at work, and different people are motivated in different ways. However, there are some general methods that can help to increase internal customer satisfaction. It is worth considering any idea that helps to encourage staff and helps them to feel worthy and valued:

- ❂ **Staff social events**
- ❂ **Financial rewards**
- ❂ **Employee of the month awards**
- ❂ **Simply saying thank you goes a long way**
- ❂ **A staff newsletter**
- ❂ **A career structure with promotion**

- ✪ **Informal praise and encouragement**
- ✪ **A performance review or appraisal**

External Customers

▼▼▼▼▼▼▼▼▼

External customers
a customer who has no direct connection with an organisation and so visits it by choice

▲▲▲▲▲▲▲▲▲

External customers are perhaps what springs to mind when the word 'customer' is mentioned. An **external customer** gets out their money and pays for a product or service at a particular place because they choose to. The first consideration is what the external customer is called. Many organisations simply use the term 'customer', although in recent years there has been a move away from this. Certainly there are more variations nowadays, including 'guests' and 'visitors'.

The aim is to make the customer feel as welcome as possible, so the new terms are designed to be more personal and welcoming. They take the emphasis away from the fact that the customer is paying for the product or service. They can also be tailored to the product or service; perhaps all riders on an alien black hole water flume may be called futuristic adventurers. Whatever you call them, external customers may be subdivided into many categories. The choice of categories may depend on several criteria:

- ✪ **The aim of the organisation**
- ✪ **The number of customers**

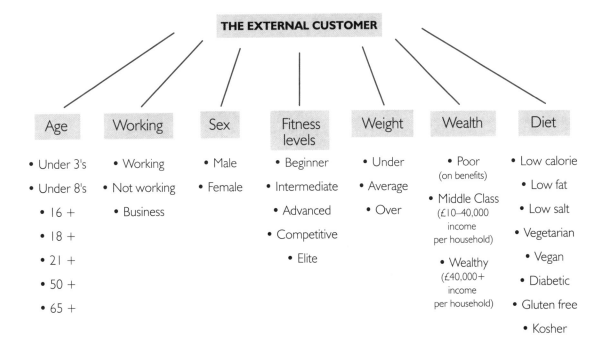

Classification of the external customer

✪ **The profile of the customers**

✪ **The type of organisation**

✪ **The size of the organisation**

✪ **The products or services sold**

And here are some possible categories:

✪ **Individual customers**
✪ **Groups of customers**
✪ **Male or female**
✪ **Different ages**
✪ **Different cultures**
✪ **Non-English-speaking customers**
✪ **Wealth**
✪ **Business customers**
✪ **Customers with specific needs**
✪ **Moaners and non-moaners**

Here are some general hints and tips:

✪ **Be careful not to offend a customer, particularly when dealing with any specific requirements such as cultural differences, language barriers, age or diet**

✪ **If you don't know something, say so then seek advice**

✪ **Honesty is both refreshing and reasonable**

✪ **Treat each person as an individual; follow the rules but be flexible enough to cope with exceptions**

✪ **Only categorise customers when it makes sense; don't do it needlessly**

The reason for classifying customers is to look at common behaviour and expectations then provide the service most people desire. It's a great technique for maximising profits, but you still need to treat people as individuals.

Age
Under 3s

Infants under 3 require special attention. There are certain legal requirements under the Children Act 1989. Besides that, under 3s require a great deal of care, attention and expertise; they need nappies, feeding and changing equipment. Plan carefully and budget adequately; under 3s can prove expensive. In terms of changing areas, the sex of the infant is irrelevant. Infants are not usually charged for a service, e.g. a swim.

Under 8s

Under 8s have the same legal protection as under 3s. They shouldn't require nappies and feeding, but they still need a great deal of care and attention. Most under 8s need action or they get bored. They may still need help when changing or going to the toilet. Generally an 8 year old boy should change in the male changing area not in the female changing area. Under 8s are usually charged at a child rate, below the adult rate.

Under 16s

Under 16s are generally categorised for pricing only. At 16 some organisations will charge adult rates.

Over 18s

Over 18, and also over 21, is often used for admission to bars, clubs and certain films. Pricing is nearly always at the adult rate.

Over 50s

Over 50s enjoy taking part in activities designed for their age range and they often receive price discounts at off-peak times. Older people can be sensitive about their age and quick to take offence, so be tactful. Two activities are swimming sessions and Saga holidays.

Concessionary and group rates

Concessionary rates or discounted rates can be given according to age. Another classification can be the lifestyle of the individual such as discounts for students or the unemployed. Activities are often designed according to age such as over 25s party nights at a nightclub or 18–30s package holidays. These classifications are based on the idea that people of a certain age like similar things. Remember, though, age classifications are not always the most successful.

Diet

Some people will only eat certain types of food, and most organisations now bear this in mind. Here are some diets that are often catered for:

- ✪ **Low-fat diets**
- ✪ **Low-calorie diets**
- ✪ **Sugar-free diets**

- **Diabetic dishes**
- **Children's menus**
- **Baby food**
- **Vegetarian dishes**
- **Kosher foods**
- **Gluten-free diets**

If food is an organisation's major attraction, it should pay special attention to dietary requirements and preferences so it can cater for as many customers as possible. At the very least, it should have an awareness of certain dietary requirements. Everyone in a food-serving area should know about diabetes, for example.

Do not offer food or drink to a child without knowing their individual requirements. There can be serious medical problems if a diabetic child drinks a sugar-laden orange drink. And there may be legal repercussions if you have offered it to them.

Gender

Most leisure centres offer activities that are male-only or female-only. There has also been the growth of single-sex leisure facilities such as the Lady in Leisure Group health clubs. This can be a way of putting on activities designed for a specific sex. The Lady in Leisure Group markets themselves as catering largely for the unfit, overweight and beginners.

Other categories

Some other categories are based on wealth; an expensive health facility will only appeal to rich people. There are activities for the overweight such as slimming groups (membership can be limited to those who are at least 3 kg overweight), the unfit, the moderately fit and the very fit and also pregnant women. Some activities may be organised for certain religious groups or for people learning English as a second language.

There has also been a growth in the number of business users in leisure and recreation. In the business world it appears to be a good idea to entertain and make money at the same time. Football clubs have large numbers of corporate or business customers and many a deal is done during a football match, particularly if the home team wins. Some business users may require more formal facilities, perhaps an impressive restaurant and well-stocked bar.

A customer can change categories during their lifetime; perhaps they were poor ten years ago and now they are rich.

Many organisations like to attract as many people as possible – the more the better. Hence groups are often actively sought after and group incentives are provided, e.g. one free admission for every 10 people at a theme park or a discounted rate for groups; the larger the group, the greater the discount.

However, some organisations do not want to attract groups, especially if they are all male or all female. Some holiday companies and theme parks will not admit all-male groups because they are seen as potential troublemakers. Some restaurants at service stations will not admit coach parties or groups.

CARICATURE OF PROFESSIONAL MOANER

Professional moaners moan about everything

Professional moaners

Professional moaners moan about everything. They want something for nothing and will only be satisfied with a full refund and perhaps financial compensation.

Most organisations dread professional moaners. They are probably the worst type of customer, although they certainly provide a challenge. If you are the member of staff dealing with them, they will try to make you feel personally responsible for their unhappiness, which is likely to be the worst you and they have ever known. They will also ensure as many people as possible know of their dilemma by talking loudly and always in public. They will know the procedures to go through and will persevere, taking photographs in evidence and formally documenting every incident.

Professional moaners need to be treated with an assertive and confident approach, and a senior member of staff probably needs to deal with them. From the organisation's viewpoint there is no room for error. The way this type of customer is treated depends on the organisation, their aims and their feelings. It might be that the organisation does not want the customer to visit again and politely asks them not to return. However, if the image of the organisation is likely to be damaged, perhaps through a newspaper article, it may be wise to adopt a different approach. The cost of a refund may be small compared to potential loss of custom through bad publicity. The member of staff needs to know how to deal with professional moaners.

Activity 5.3

★ Study your classmates or a group of friends. If you had to place these friends into customer types, how would you go about it? What types of customer would you identify? How does the group benefit from having a classification?

★ Visit a leisure and recreation venue and collect the programme of activities on offer. List the customer types identified by the venue and discuss why you think this was done. Do you agree with it? What changes would you make?

Selling skills

Selling is about persuading the customer to purchase a product. There's more to it than getting someone to part with their cash. Selling is a lengthy process and it can be done in several ways. This section looks at how to sell things in leisure and recreation. Let's begin with some aims; selling tries to:

- ✪ **Create an awareness of a product**
- ✪ **Encourage sales**
- ✪ **Enhance reputation**
- ✪ **Encourage repeat custom**
- ✪ **Encourage new customers**

The emphasis of these aims may vary according to the product being sold and the aims of the organisation. A profit-making organisation in the private sector may put more emphasis on sales targets, whereas a non-profit organisation may be more interested in repeat customers. Nowadays all organisations should aim to achieve sales through better customer service, so the historical differences between commercial and non-commercial hardly exist any longer. The aims of selling can be achieved by:

- ✪ **Sales promotion**
    discount vouchers
    trial offers
    multi-buys
- ✪ **Direct selling conducted person-to-person**
- ✪ **Indirect selling through the post and over the internet**
- ✪ **Sales techniques such as hard sell and soft sell**
- ✪ **After-sales care**

A sale can be broken down into four stages:

- ✪ *Raising initial customer awareness*: **customers need to be told that a product or service is available. Advertising and promotions are essential here**
- ✪ *Developing this interest*: **customers want to find out more information before making a purchase. Personal selling and careful negotiations are the keys to this. Use a hard sell, a soft sell or something in between (Table 5.1). Most organisations go for a soft sell as a hard sell rarely achieves repeat customers or enhanced reputation. This is certainly true of leisure and recreation**
- ✪ *Closing the sale*: **having decided to buy, customers will go ahead and complete the transaction. Don't do anything to discourage them. Use all your interpersonal skills and remain subtly persuasive**
- ✪ *After sales*: **immediately after the sale, customers may decide to buy guarantees and extended warranties. This aspect is mainly covered by policies but front-line staff should be familiar with them**

Hard sell	Soft sell
Pressurises the customer	Allows the customer to make a choice
Presents biased information	Advises the customer in a balanced way
Uninterested in the needs of the customer	Assesses the needs of the customer
	Aims to meet these needs
Sole aim is to maximise financial gain	Comprehensive after-sales service
Minimal or no after-sales service	

Table 5.1   *Hard sell versus soft sell*

Sales and selling can be split into strategy and operations. Strategy covers planning, direction and focus. This is where decisions are made and plans are formulated to achieve an organisation's aims and objectives. Strategy is usually worked out by senior managers. The workforce then carries out this strategy as operations. The workforce includes sales assistants, sales supervisors and other front-line staff. Operational matters include staffing levels and sales targets.

The leisure and recreation industry uses personal selling to sell many of its services. A large number of sales are achieved through trust and reputation built up through the skill and expertise of the sales staff. But in the end, selling involves everybody. Without a conscientious cleaner to freshen your surroundings, who would see your subtle sales technique? Here are some jobs and activities that involve sales:

- **Greeting customers**
- **Advising customers**
- **Comments and complaints**
- **Taking orders**
- **Demonstrating products**
- **Giving presentations**
- **Health, safety and security**
- **Describing services**
- **Taking payment**
- **Delivery of products**
- **After-sales services**
- **Stock control**

Not all sales jobs involve all these aspects, and different aspects will occur with different frequencies. A sales assistant that delivers a product is unlikely to take orders, whereas a sales assistant that presents an exhibition is likely to. Some sales assistants will not deal with customer complaints, they will pass them on to management immediately. A lifeguard will give advice to customers and they are certainly concerned with health and safety, but they will not handle payments. To be successful in sales you need to demonstrate the following characteristics:

- **Friendly attitude**
- **Reassuring manner**
- **Product knowledge**
- **Industry knowledge**
- **Energy and enthusiasm**
- **Faith in your product**
- **Subtle persuasion**
- **A smart appearance**
- **Discretion**
- **Time management**

Sales and selling need to be considered as part of the overall marketing plan. The methods chosen and the policies adopted should be in line with the overall aims and objectives of the organisation.

Activity
5.4

Split into groups of three

Identify a product or service in the leisure and recreation industry

Plan how to sell it using a hard sell and a soft sell

Role-play the soft sell. One person can be the customer, one can be the salesperson and one can be an observer

Keep the same roles but this time play out the hard sell

The observer should then lead a discussion to analyse your findings

Dealing with customers

Dealing with customers is quite easy; dealing with them successfully may be harder. Most people working in the leisure and recreation industry will have some contact with customers. This does not have to be direct contact; it may be indirectly through a job that they do. Suppose you asked swimming pool customers to specify the two most important aspects of customer service, most would say that the water must be warm and the pool must be clean. The customer service here is provided by the maintenance engineer and the cleaner. Both may have little direct contact with customers but the work they do on the pool could be the difference between delight and disappointment.

Everyone in an organisation should know how to deal with customers successfully even if there's no obvious need. How many times have you asked someone a question just because they wear a uniform? For example, a lifeguard could get asked the price of an aerobics session even though it has nothing to do with their job.

Communication is an integral part of dealing with customers. Try to communicate an appropriate message in an appropriate way and give the customer some appropriate satisfaction. Contact with customers can happen in many ways:

- **Face-to-face or in person**
- **On the telephone**
- **In writing**
    letter

    memo

    fax

    email
- **Website**
- **Newsletter**
- **Noticeboard**
- **Non-verbal communication**
- **Marketing material**
    posters

    leaflets

    tickets

Empathy
seeing something from someone else's viewpoint; treating someone the way you'd like to be treated yourself

It is so difficult to know exactly what the customer wants. We can only try to get as close as possible. The key to this is **empathy**. Besides empathy, there are some golden rules that can help. They apply whatever the customer and whatever the method of communication.

- ✪ Assess the message from the customer; this may mean listening to the customer or reading an email carefully, but make sure the message has been clearly understood
- ✪ Don't assume anything about anyone
- ✪ Ensure the language is appropriate for the customer, apply the **KISS** principle (see page 222) and use plain English
- ✪ Always be polite and courteous
- ✪ Always think how you'd like to be treated yourself. If you were the customer, what would you want to happen?
- ✪ Always remain calm
- ✪ Never lose your temper in speech or in writing
- ✪ Be objective and stick to the facts
- ✪ Know what you're talking about or get some advice
- ✪ Be positive in your speech and your body language
- ✪ Always respond in a way that your organisation wants you to
- ✪ Choose an appropriate degree of formality

Some customer situations

Dealing with a customer face-to-face

- ✪ Smile and listen
- ✪ Look but don't stare
- ✪ Maintain your interest
    - Don't glance away
    - Don't talk to other people
- ✪ Address the customer by name
- ✪ Don't interrupt the customer
- ✪ Don't try to finish their sentences
- ✪ Don't stand too close to the customer
- ✪ Finish by agreeing what will happen now
- ✪ Always say thank you

Dealing with a customer on the phone

✪ **Answer the telephone within four rings but not before two rings. After one ring suggests the organisation isn't busy enough. After five rings suggest it's inefficient**

✪ **If the incoming call needs to be put on hold, ensure the customer cannot overhear any conversations**

✪ **When you answer the phone, tell the customer the name of your organisation. Greet them politely like this: 'Good morning, Newtown Leisure Centre. How can I help you?' Try to speak naturally; no sing-song voices**

DEALING WITH A CUSTOMER ON THE TELEPHONE

Room for Improvement	Good
answered after two rings customer perceives this as inefficient	answered with 4 rings just right
Hello the customer does not know if they have the right number	Good morning, Newtown Leisure Centre. Can I help you? customer knows they have got through to the right place
Is that Newtown Leisure Centre?	
Yes	
Is the manager there please?	Can I speak to the manager please? well mannered
No no alternatives offered	Sorry she is not in the leisure centre at moment, can the duty officer help?
When can I speak to her please?	No I would like to speak to the manager please
Don't know, try later on if you want Bye No pleasant end to the call	Can I take your name and number please? She will call you back before 4 o'clock, is that O.K.? offers an alternative
Customer is unhappy with call and no closer to speaking to the manager	Yes, thank you Thanks for calling Goodbye Pleasant finish
	Customer satisfied they will get a response

Smile on the phone: it does make a difference

THE TEN COMMANDMENTS OF CUSTOMER SERVICE

1. WE WILL ALWAYS GREET CUSTOMERS WITH A SMILE

2. WE WILL BE CARING AND COURTEOUS AT ALL TIMES

3. WE WILL NEVER SAY NO, AND WILL ALWAYS STRIVE TO OFFER AN ALTERNATIVE IF THE CUSTOMER'S REQUEST IS NOT AVAILABLE

4. WE WILL USE THE CUSTOMER'S NAME, ONCE IDENTIFIED

5. WE WILL ALWAYS BE SMART IN APPEARANCE

6. THE PRODUCT WE SERVE WILL ALWAYS BE CONSISTENT, RELIABLE AND OF HIGH QUALITY

7. WE WILL LISTEN TO THE CUSTOMER AND RESPOND IMMEDIATELY TO THEIR NEEDS

8. WE WILL KNOW THE VILLAGE PRODUCT

9. WE WILL NEVER WALK PAST A QUALITY PROBLEM

10. WE WILL HANDLE COMPLAINTS WITH CONCERN TO RESOLVING THE PROBLEM

Follow these ten commandments

- **Speak clearly over the telephone and don't mumble**
- **Sometimes a customer may speak to you because the person they need is unavailable. Take down their message and pass it to the relevant person (see page 214)**
- **Smile – you can hear a smile on the telephone**

Dealing with a customer in writing

There are several ways of writing to customers. A formal letter may be the best way to contact external customers, whereas a handwritten message may be quite acceptable for internal customers. It depends on what you want to say. Here are some of the options:

- **Letter**
- **Fax**
- **Email**
- **Memo**
- **Poster**
- **Noticeboard**
- **Staff handbook**

- ✪ **Leaflet**
- ✪ **Message**
- ✪ **Record card**

Here are some rules for any written message:

- ✪ **It should be spelt and punctuated correctly**
- ✪ **It should have a beginning, middle and end**
- ✪ **It should be accurate and effective**
- ✪ **It should be clear who it's to and who it's from**
- ✪ **It should be clear when it was sent and what it's about**
- ✪ **It should look pleasing to the eye**
- ✪ **It should use appropriate language**

DEALING WITH A CUSTOMER IN WRITING

Room for improvement

To Paul
from Peter

Please mend the rowing machine

No detail: which machine?
by when? who repairs it?
and no date

Good

MEMO

To: Paul Walker, Fitness Suite Supervisor
From: Peter Arnold, Leisure Centre Manager
Re: Repair to Rowing Machine (4) in
        Fitness Suite
Date: 09/01/00

As discussed, please arrange for the rowing machine
to be repaired.
The manufacturer will repair it without charge as it
is still under guarantee. Please contact Roger Malt at
Training Enc. on 0171 625 439 to arrange the details.
I am assured this repair can be completed within 5 days.
Please contact me if you have any problems.
Thanks, Peter.

Factual
Offers a solution
Offers support
Dated and titled

There are several ways of writing to customers

Needs improving

Membership cards

Name: Jane Alsop
Address: 21 Film Rd
Telephone number: 615111
Details: Fun member

Insufficient details,
the address isn't full,
neither is the telephone
number. How does the
member pay?

A good example

Flounders Squash Club

Membership Details

Name: Jane Alsop
Address: 21 Film Rd, Dring, Yorkshire YR5 2LU
Telephone number -   Day: 0942 615111
                     Evening: 0193 641233
Membership Number:
Gold ☑   Silver ☐   Casual ☐

Payment method
Direct ☑   Invoice ☐   Invoice ☐
Debit   Monthly   Quarterly

Comprehensive details

**Records can be kept on a computer data base or on manual record card.
The information needs to be ordered and relevant**

A Message

Room for improvement	**A good example**

To: Ian

Call Julie please

What does
Julie want?

When should Ian
call back?

Scrappy bit of paper –
likely to get lost

When was the message
taken?

Message Taken

To: Ian
From: Julie
Date: 3/12/99 Time: 11.30am

☐ Will call again   ☐ Returning your call
☑ Please call back   ☑ Left a message

Message:
Have you got the staffing rotas for over Christmas?
Please could you call to discuss by Friday noon.
Thanks.

It is clear who the message is for, when it was taken and what needs to be done.

Dealing with a customer over the internet

In the past year or so, there has been a marked increase in the number of organisations communicating over the internet – via websites and through email. This trend is likely to continue. The internet is a fairly new marketing tool in the UK but many organisations now use it. Email makes it harder to pretend things got lost in the post. Electronic naggers can be set to repeat the original message, perhaps weekly, until a response is received.

Some organisations like dealing over the internet, others are reluctant. Some organisations continually redesign their websites, others have yet to build one. Some websites have email feedback, others are not much more than adverts. Customers may feel frustrated if they cannot email their feedback. Bear this in mind whenever you design a website.

Communication through email tends to be quite informal; you can treat emails like handwritten messages on computer. And this informality comes with tremendous power. You can attach documents and demos to show the customer your product before they buy. Another way is to build virtual tours into your website. While Derby County was completing its new football stadium at Pride Park, supporters could take a virtual tour before buying a season ticket. They could even try out different seats.

To stay competitive, organisations will almost certainly have to serve their customers over the internet. Many customers like to send emails, and without a proper internet strategy, organisations can be overwhelmed by this feedback.

Other aspects of customer service

Here's a list

- ❂ **Providing information**
- ❂ **Giving advice**
- ❂ **Taking and relaying messages (page 214)**
- ❂ **Keeping records (page 213)**
- ❂ **Providing assistance**
- ❂ **Dealing with problems**
- ❂ **Handling complaints**
- ❂ **Offering extra services**

Providing information

When customers ask for information, make your replies relevant, accurate and useful. It's unreasonable if customers expect you to know everything about all subjects. But it's not unreasonable if they demand a certain level of knowledge. For example, a pool attendant should know about activities in the gym but they needn't have full details. We can look at two sorts of information: information about the organisation and information about products and services.

Information about the organisation

Every organisation has unique rules, regulations and expectations. Internal customers, or employees, can find them in their staff handbook. For external customers, many organisations produce a **mission statement** and a **customer care policy**. Here's a mission statement for Newtown Leisure Centre:

▼ ▼ ▼ ▼ ▼ ▼ ▼ ▼ ▼

Mission statement
a broad declaration that tells the customer what to expect

Customer care policy
tells the customer specifically what they can expect

▲ ▲ ▲ ▲ ▲ ▲ ▲ ▲ ▲

THE SUCCESSFUL PROVIDER OF CUSTOMER SERVICE

Bright new ideas

clear voice, talks to the customers, a friendly approach

excellent product knowledge and organisational knowledge

appropriate make-up

a friendly smile

no nail polish, appropriate jewellery (particularly where food is!)

punctual, flexible, available

name badge for identification

loyal to the organisation

company uniform

suitable dress

Learns from mistake (once = mistake twice = foolish!)

takes initiative

suitable footwear

MULTI FUNCTIONAL

Customer service: people with initiative provide it properly

Newtown Leisure Centre aims to improve the standard and quality of leisure for all residents and visitors of Newtown. This is through provision of a wide range of leisure opportunities that are affordable and available to all sections of the community. To help achieve this, all staff at Newtown are committed to this aim and are trained to provide the highest standards of customer care.

CUSTOMER CARE POLICY

AIMS

To ensure that customers enjoy their visit, want to return and spread the word that The Dome, and its staff, cares.

To reduce the level of complaints to the stage where only those incidents occur which are beyond the control of staff, or are accidental.

Mission statement

All members of The Dome's staff are committed to serving customers as specified in the Customer Care Charter.

The aim is to ensure that customers enjoy their visit, want to return and spread the word that The Dome, and its staff, cares.

The Doncaster Dome aims to be a caring leisure park
(Courtesy The Dome, Doncaster Leisure Management)

There is nothing specific and measurable in this statement; it highlights the direction of the organisation and allows the customer to have some idea about what they can expect. A customer care policy is much more specific; it tells the customer exactly what they can expect and how these expectations are measured. In other words, an organisation meets the customer's needs or it doesn't. Here is part of the policy for Newtown Leisure Centre:

At Newtown Leisure Centre we are committed to providing a high-quality service every time you visit our centre. We promise you that:

★   *The time and availability of activities will be published in the customer information leaflet*
★   *Any changes will be displayed on the main noticeboard*
★   *The swimming pool will be heated to 28 C; it will be clean and safe to use and it will be supervised by sufficient and qualified staff*
★   *The vending machines will be fully stocked*
★   *Staff will be easy to recognise, suitably dressed in uniform and with name badges*
★   *Everyone will be treated equally*

Here it is easy for an external customer and the member of staff to assess the performance of Newtown Leisure Centre; these statements are either achieved or they're not. They offer a target to the member of staff and should quantify what the organisation sees as successful customer service. This is important because these goals need to be clear so that every member of staff knows exactly what to do when they're on duty. The mission statement and the customer care policy are often widely publicised so all customers know about them and realise the organisation takes them seriously.

Sometimes the organisation will fail to meet the demands of the mission statement and the customer care policy. The reasons for this failure may be beyond its control. For example, a boiler breakdown may not be discovered until 30 minutes before an early-riser swimming session. This means the water will be colder than the specified 28 C. A ride at a theme park may have to be shut because of a fault on a safety mechanism. Most customers are understanding and will accept valid reasons, but they need to be told as soon as possible. Any delay and you'll be flooded with complaints.

To achieve the highest standards of customer service, here are some aspects to include in the staff handbook and the customer care policy:

- **The specific aims of the organisation**
- **The complaints procedure**
- **After-sales**

Information about products and services

All members of staff working in an organisation are likely to have strengths and weaknesses; they are likely to know more about some areas than others. This is perfectly reasonable. If a member of staff is a specialist, they are expected to know a lot about this specialism; if the member of staff is a generalist, they are expected to know a small amount about lots of different areas. No one is expected to know everything.

A receptionist should know opening times, prices, directions, who does what, and so on. They are unlikely to know the steps in a pool test, the cardiovascular benefits of exercise or the average body fat in a 25 year old woman.

All members of staff should have an overview of what happens in their place of work. It also helps if you know what's happening in the local area, what your competitors may be doing and what's happening in the industry as a whole. Knowledgeable staff make a difference and give organisations an advantage. But no one can know everything.

In conclusion, a member of staff needs to have a thorough understanding of how the organisation operates, what products and services it offers and what the customer can reasonably expect. Then they should be able to deal successfully with customers from the moment they walk through the door to the moment they hand over payment.

Giving advice

- ✪ **Always let the customer make their own choice**
- ✪ **Always stick to the facts**
- ✪ **Meet the customer's needs, not your own**
- ✪ **Do what is best for the customer and for the organisation**
- ✪ **Provide a balanced view then let the customer decide:**

    > This shoe has been designed for the middle-distance road runner

    > This shoe has a cushioning system that's just been introduced

Providing assistance

Customers often tell the tale of walking into a shop and being pounced on by the sales assistant. This puts many people off, never to return. Sometimes customers welcome assistance, sometimes they shy away. Try to read their signs and offer appropriate assistance at the right moment. Customers expect attention when:

- ✪ **They want to pay**
- ✪ **They have a question**
- ✪ **They want to make a comment**

Customers expect to be left alone when:

- ✪ **They want to browse**
- ✪ **They want to talk to someone with them**
- ✪ **They know what they want and where to find it**

Look for signals that show whether the customer wants assistance. Non-verbal communication or body language is a useful guide in these situations. Often these signals are obvious; perhaps the customer asks for help, or perhaps they look around for a sales assistant. If you are on the telephone, acknowledge customers who are waiting in person, otherwise they may leave, especially if they're in a hurry or they're looking after young children. Try to be available but not overpowering.

Offering extra services

Many believe it's the extras that sell a product. Providing that little bit more service can encourage a customer to be loyal forever. In other words, the things they don't expect are the things that draw them back.

These extras may be a very helpful person on the telephone, or a member of staff talking to a child in a particularly friendly and understanding way, or complimentary towels and shampoo at a health club. There are endless opportunities and all of them are important.

Extra services may also provide an opportunity to increase profits. For example, most cinemas make a great deal of money out of sweets, ice creams and other refreshments when their main business is selling tickets to watch films. The same applies to leisure centres; often as much money is spent in the vending machines as in the swimming pool – its main service.

Activity 5.5

Visit a leisure and recreation facility. Find out their mission statement and their customer care policies. Then consider these questions:

★ Were they displayed?

★ As a customer, do you feel they are satisfactory?

★ If you were the employer, would you feel they were satisfactory?

★ How does the service measure up?

Handling complaints

The leisure and recreation industry is built on what we choose to do in our leisure time. In many respects it's a great industry to work in because no one is forced to take part unless they want to. People doing their leisure activities are often in a good mood, so if something does go wrong, they may be less likely to complain. That means, compared with other industries, leisure and recreation should receive fewer complaints. But nowadays more and more people are happy to say what they think; customers are more aware of their rights, they expect more and they want to see action if their needs are not met.

The term 'complaint' has negative implications; it suggests there is something wrong. On many occasions members of the public want to pass comment on a product or service they have experienced. The term 'comment' is neither negative nor positive. If you ask for complaints, many people will rack their brains to think of something that was wrong. We do tend to concentrate on the bad bits. Inviting customers to complain is negative and generates an unnecessary workload. If you ask for complaints, have no doubt, you'll get them! Inviting customers to comment is inviting them to praise and perhaps give a little constructive criticism. People are less likely to try to find something to moan about, so your overall complaints should go down and the ones that are left should be genuine. These complaints may reveal important things about your business.

Customers tend to complain because their needs are not met; they tend not to comment if their needs are met; and they tend to give praise if their expectations are exceeded. For a member of staff to achieve this little bit extra, they have to be aware of exactly what they're expected to provide. This information is usually provided in staff training but also in the customer care policy and the staff handbook. If the staff handbook is comprehensive it will probably have a section that gives some hints on how to deal with a customer who has a complaint.

There are many ways of receiving customer comments; the later sections of this unit study this in more detail. However, customer complaints can be received in the following ways:

✪ **In person**
✪ **By letter**
✪ **By email**
✪ **By phone**
✪ **By fax**
✪ **By feedback**

No matter how the comments are received, the golden rules remain the same:

✪ **Listen or read carefully**
✪ **If positive say thank you**
✪ **If negative say sorry that their expectations have not been met**
✪ **Assess the situation**
✪ **Investigate the claims but be tactful**
✪ **Don't suggest that you doubt the customer**
✪ **If necessary offer a solution**
✪ **If necessary agree a solution**
✪ **Give the customer a timescale**
✪ **Tell the staff concerned**
✪ **If you've made a mistake, admit it**
✪ **Pass on any compliments to relevant staff**

- ✪ **If criticisms are made communicate them sensitively, everyone makes mistakes**
- ✪ **Solve problems so they don't recur**
- ✪ **Always finish on a positive note**

Keep
It
Simple and
Safe

To avoid the message being misinterpreted

Exercise 5.2

Choose a facility or organisation where you have been a customer and think about how you have been dealt with:

★ on the telephone

★ face to face

★ as part of a group

★ in writing

From these experiences choose a good and a bad situation and state what you would do and why if you were providing the service.

Most organisations will have a specified customer comments procedure; this will allow comments to be registered, actioned and reviewed in a planned manner. It will also allow the organisation to gather standard feedback and allow customers to add remarks of their own. This procedure should ensure that the golden rules are adhered to. See pages 223–8 for more detail on gathering customer feedback plus a few examples.

Aggressive customers

Aggressive customers can be difficult to deal with, and in extreme circumstances they can even threaten the safety of staff and other people. Here is what to do if a customer is aggressive:

- ✪ **Remain calm**

    If you remain calm, the shouter may feel foolish and then stop

- ✪ **Ask them politely not to shout**

- ✪ **Remain objective**

In the face of abuse, just repeat the facts and nothing else

○ **Apologise and explain**

Say you're sorry not to have satisfied their expectations

○ **Tell them what they can expect and when they can expect it**

○ **Close the conversation if they refuse to listen**

○ **Ask for help if you feel threatened or otherwise in need**

○ **Call the police if customers are violent**

Activity 5.6

In a group discuss a situation where you complained or you wanted to complain. What was the reason for your complaint and how did people handle it? From all the situations discussed, choose one that was resolved successfully and one that wasn't. Present them to the group.

A customer complaint is an opportunity to change a dissatisfied customer into a satisfied customer. If a complaint is resolved in a simple and structured way, a customer may remember it and feel secure that future issues will be dealt with smoothly.

Assessing service quality

Let's return to our familiar starting point: customer service is about meeting the needs of the customer and trying to provide that little bit extra. As each customer is unique and has different expectations, it's not an easy task. It's in the interests of any organisation to find out as much as it can about its customers. The more relevant the information, the more likely it can satisfy its customers.

When an organisation draws up a business plan, it usually collects this sort of information so it can test whether its project is worthwhile. But once the project is under way, the feelings of the customer need to be monitored continually; they need to be reassessed and the plans changed accordingly. We all know that our likes and dislikes change over time. Many customers also like to voice their opinions and they feel valued if they are asked in the first place.

Gathering and measuring customer service is based on the fact that everyone and everything has room for improvement. No one is perfect, so all of us should be happy to listen to suggestions and view them as a way to greater success. Here are three questions to help us:

✪ **Does the customer like what they are getting now?**

✪ **What changes would they like to see?**

✪ **Why would they like to see these changes?**

What is useful information?

It is useful to know the reasons behind customer choice as sometimes the customer wants something but is unlikely ever to get it or use it; these are called false needs. For example, some customers may like to see a leisure club with health and beauty facilities but they themselves would never use them. False needs have to be viewed with caution, else you may be providing a service that few people will buy.

The information you gather is really only as useful as the questions that prompt it. It is relatively easy to find out whether or not customers are happy; you can ask them or you can study the sales figures. If the figures are increasing or decreasing, this can broadly equate to customer satisfaction or dissatisfaction.

So it can make improvements, an organisation needs to know two specific things about its customers: what's making them happy and what would make them happier. Closed questions – Are you happy with our service, yes or no? – may tell an organisation they need to improve but that's about all. Here's a more specific question that might be better:

How would you describe the temperature of our pool?

★ *Too hot*
★ *Just right*
★ *Too cold*

This provides much more information. It tells the organisation exactly what its customers think of the pool temperature. So decide what information you need, devise some questions to help you obtain it then structure them in a logical order that's easy for your customers. There are five main methods of gathering customer service information:

✪ **Informal feedback**

✪ **Surveys**

✪ **Suggestion boxes or schemes**

✪ **Focus groups**

✪ **Mystery shoppers or audits**

✪ **Observation**

Informal feedback

▼▼▼▼▼▼▼▼▼

Informal feedback
information gathered without any detailed plan or structure and often just by chatting to customers, both internal and external

▲▲▲▲▲▲▲▲▲

The best way to gather **informal feedback** is by striking up a conversation and asking a variety of open-ended questions. Open-ended questions are those that encourage a lengthy and informative response. Here are some examples:

- ✪ **What do you think of the newly refurbished gym?**
- ✪ **How would you improve the booking system for the squash courts?**
- ✪ **Tell me about the new bar menu?**

This method of gathering information is useful; it gives the organisation a feel for a service and how it is doing. It also provides hints and ideas on how to make improvements. But the responses should be viewed with caution; they do not necessarily give a balanced view; you are gathering opinions and beliefs that may not be factual or representative of the whole range of customers. This feedback is opinion. Informal feedback is only a guide to the level of customer satisfaction.

Surveys

▼▼▼▼▼▼▼▼▼

Survey
a structured and planned method of gathering information, often using a series of specific questions

▲▲▲▲▲▲▲▲▲

We will concentrate on the questionnaire **survey**. A questionnaire aims to provide a clear measure of a situation, e.g. customer satisfaction. This information needs to be specific and useful. An organisation needs to know what makes its customers happy but it also needs to know how happy they are. This is often measured by a scoring system. Here are two examples:

How would you describe the speed at which your meal was served?
excellent ❑ *good* ❑ *average* ❑ *poor* ❑ *very poor* ❑

How do you rate the cleanliness of our changing areas?
excellent ❑ *good* ❑ *average* ❑ *poor* ❑ *very poor* ❑

The questionnaire itself should be split into four parts. The first part is an introduction; this should include a title, a short explanation of what the customer needs to do and why they are doing it. Here is an example:

HELPING US TO HELP YOU

Thank you for taking the time and effort to answer the following questions. They will help us to improve the service we provide to you. If you need any assistance please ask at the reception of Flounders Squash Club.

The second part should ask the specific questions that are quantified or measured by a scoring system, just as we have explored. The third part should invite the customer to add comments in their own way and their own words. The fourth area should say what will happen with the information and should end by thanking the customer. Here is an example:

This information will now be passed to the general manager of Flounders

Squash Club. If you would like a reply, please complete the details below (if your name and address has not already been collected). Thank you for helping Flounders Squash Club to help you.

Here are a few hints to help you with questionnaires:

- ✪ **Use suitable language and keep it simple**
- ✪ **Use please and thank you; be polite**
- ✪ **Provide pens; not all customers carry them**
- ✪ **Ask just a few questions, not hundreds**

Carsington Water

Please tell us what you think!

We hope that you have enjoyed your visit. We always welcome feedback from our visitors and we would like to know your views on the facilities here at Carsington Water. Please write your comments, together with a few details about you and your party, in the space below. Your details will help us provide the facilities you want.

Name (Mr/Mrs/Ms/Miss) _____

Home Town _____ Date of visit _____

Age _____ Number in party _____

Comments _____
_____
_____
_____
_____
_____
_____

Is this your first visit to Carsington Water? (please tick):   Yes ☐   No ☐

How has this visit affected your impression of Severn Trent? (tick one):
For the better ☐   No change ☐   For the worse ☐

Thank you for your help.
Please return to the reception desk in the foyer.

Severn Trent Water

ST.5973

Carsington Water has over 1.2 million visitors a year
(Courtesy Severn Trent Water Ltd)

- ✪ **Make it fun, perhaps with smileys**
- ✪ **Offer other feedback to people who don't read or write**
- ✪ **Collect names and addresses if you can**
- ✪ **Remember the Data Protection Act**

Suggestion boxes or schemes

Suggestion boxes or schemes sometimes operate to collect questionnaires or comment cards. They can take a structured form such as a questionnaire or an unstructured form that invites free comments. They give the customer an opportunity to make comments and place them in a box, often positioned close to the exit or in a reception area. Suggestion cards are set out like questionnaires:

- ✪ **Introduction**
- ✪ **Main set of questions**
- ✪ **Customer comments**
- ✪ **Thank you**

Remember to empty the boxes and reply to the suggestions. It's easy to overlook them until they overflow. By then they may be full of comments saying how slow you are to send a reply.

Focus groups

▼▼▼▼▼▼▼▼▼

Focus group
a group of people who meet to exchange views and ideas

▲▲▲▲▲▲▲▲▲

A few customers may be brought together in a **focus group** to discuss a series of topics; a lead person will then collate feedback, hints and ideas. Be careful with focus group information; similar to informal feedback, it is the opinion of just a few customers. For focus groups to be successful, they need to represent a wide range of customers but they have to be small enough for everyone to be heard. A suitable number would be between 12 and 20.

Mystery shoppers or audits

▼▼▼▼▼▼▼▼▼

Mystery shopper
someone who visits a facility on behalf of its owner to assess the customer service without the staff knowing

▲▲▲▲▲▲▲▲▲

The leisure and recreation industry is sending out **mystery shoppers** more and more. The aim is to get a truer picture of customer service than by sending people who are known assessors. The mystery shopper will have a set of criteria to work from. They will probably be scored like a questionnaire.

The whole process aims to see customer service from a customer's viewpoint. It allows real situations to be assessed. Mystery shoppers check the service at Harry Ramsden's fish and chip restaurants and at UCI cinemas. The staff receive feedback and there are financial rewards when their service is excellent.

What do you do with useful information?

Once the information has been gathered, it should be absorbed and considered then an action plan should be put together. Try to improve your customer service so the bad bits don't happen again, the mediocre bits can be improved and the best bits get even better.

Gather information in as many ways as you can, so you get a balanced view of your customer service. Using just one method may leave some parts untouched. The more information you gather, the more improvements you can make and the better your service should become; sales are likely to increase and then more profit can be generated. But your information has got to be useful and relevant.

Who do you get this information from?

To get a balanced view, collect information from a cross-section of customers:

✪ **Regular customers**

✪ **New customers**

✪ **Specific customer types**

> men
>
> women
>
> over 50
>
> non-English-speaking

✪ **Internal customers (staff)**

✪ **Non-users**

Non-users are particularly important but they are often neglected. If we don't know who they are, it may be difficult to ask them why they don't use our facility. But we can contact customers on a waiting list, perhaps people who missed a swimming lesson, or we can send local people a questionnaire on how they use our facility.

The non-users can also provide valuable insight into what competitors may be doing. Perhaps we will find that 50% of parents send their children to a local competitor because its pool seems to have warmer water. We could raise our pool temperature, tell our customers and win them back, changing a negative situation into a positive.

Observation

Simply standing by and watching what customers do can be a useful way to obtain information. Although likely to be informal, it can be made more formal by scheduling observations at regular times on regular days. The observations should be treated like informal feedback and the results of focus groups. Not all the information is valid and it may not be representative. A swimmer who looks annoyed and angry may have found the water cold and the pool crowded, or they may have forgotten their towel and be running late. To produce an accurate picture, combine your observations with other information.

Finally, remember that many customers do not comment or complain, they simply vote with their feet. By gathering and measuring customer feedback in a balanced and relevant way, an organisation can help to influence its future and maximise its customers that are loyal forever.

Activity 5.7

Visit three leisure and recreation venues. How does each one gather customer feedback?

In your opinion which venue gathered the information in the best way? Justify your choice.

Fitness

James is 18 and plans to join the police force; he needs to increase his levels of fitness and so he decides to join a gym. He telephones for a free induction and the staff book him in. They explain that the induction takes place over two sessions, each lasting about 40 minutes and with a three-day break between them. They also ask why James wants to join the gym, so that his fitness programme can be tailored to his individual needs.

When James attends the first session he is assigned a member of staff who fills in a medical form. This tells them

continued

continued

about any medical history which could affect James' abilities and it helps them to ensure his safety. He is then shown around the gym and how to use the equipment properly. His fitness is comprehensively assessed and the exercises are demonstrated to help James in his aims.

The two inductions have a three-day break between them; this allows James to recover so his fitness is correctly assessed. The second session considers James' need to build up his strength, so it concentrates on weight training. Specific advice is given on how to avoid injury. James is so impressed by this attention that he joins the gym for a year. He tells lots of his friends and two of them decide to join with him. Through one opportunity the staff at the gym have:

★ Demonstrated product and organisational knowledge

★ Achieved customer satisfaction

★ Achieved customer retention

★ Gained potential new customers

Reception

Two health clubs operate within the same area, one is part of a national chain, Fitness Forever, and the other is a smaller local company, Fitness Now. Several smaller clubs in the region have recently gone out of business; this has been blamed on new openings by the national chains. Tom, who runs Fitness Now, doesn't want to be another statistic.

So Tom decides to examine the operation of Fitness Now. He decides that the facilities are not as clean as they could be; the reception area is often grubby and smoking is allowed. The telephone often takes eight rings to be

continued

continued

answered and the booking system is unreliable. There have been a number of customer complaints about this in the last two months.

Tom decides this is an ideal opportunity to change for the better. After several discussions and training sessions, he makes the following decisions:

★ The whole gym will be given a one-off overnight clean

★ A more thorough cleaning rota will then be implemented

★ Fitness Now will become no smoking

★ Calls will be answered promptly, with a target of four rings

★ A computerised booking system will be installed

★ All staff will be briefed on successful customer service

★ A customer comment system will be established

Although Fitness Now will never be as big as Fitness Forever, it will offer value for money and this can only help in the profitability of the business. Tom's plan helped to:

★ Achieve customer satisfaction

★ Enhance the image and reputation of the company

★ Provide a more efficient, consistent and reliable service

Activity 5.8

You are the customer service manager at your local Premiership football club. You have a problem to deal with. A season ticket holder is unhappy. She has spent £350 on a season ticket for herself and a season ticket for her 9 year old son, who's football crazy. She specifically asked to be seated in a respectable area and was told her seats were where the 'riff-raff' wouldn't go.

But two rows in front is a man who swears loudly and crudely throughout the game, he smokes and stands up, blocking the boy's view. And the football is awful too. No other season tickets are available. What do you do and what are the results of your action?

Revision questions

1 Define customer service.

2 Define successful customer service.

3 What is a service industry?

4 What are loyal forever customers?

5 What is the effect of good customer service?

6 Describe what is meant by appropriate dress?

7 What is non-verbal communication?

8 List five types of customer.

9 What is an internal customer?

10 What is an external customer?

11 Describe the professional moaner.

12 List five rules when dealing with customers.

13 Define empathy.

14 What is a mission statement?

15 List five methods of gathering information from customers.

16 List five characteristics of an effective telephone call.

17 List five characteristics of an effective customer service letter.

Newtown Leisure Centre

Newtown Leisure Centre makes its staff and customers the centre of attention. Believing themselves to be good listeners, the centre's management foresee a bright future. Every year a small group of staff update three documents:

★ Staff handbook
★ Mission statement
★ Customer care policy

Find an example for each of these documents then go through this updating process. Include the following details:

★ What customer service is
★ What its benefits are
★ Why you feel it's important
★ How to handle customers
★ How to handle customer comments
★ How to gather customer information

Include lots of examples from the leisure and recreation industry to support your statements.

Leisure and recreation in action

6

Objectives

- **Prepare a business plan of your project**
- **Assess the feasibility of your project**
- **Work as part of a team**
- **Apply your project practically**
- **Evaluate the success of your project**

This unit is the final putting together of all the other five. There is not much new information but you still need to think carefully as you put your knowledge into action. Much of this unit is based on a project of your choice, and you will actually get to do things.

Unlike the other units, there are no activities for you to complete, instead there are boxes called Tasks. You've already studied the theory of the leisure and recreation industry, and these boxes will help you put it into practice.

Some background

This unit may well be the most demanding and challenging of all. But it can also be the most rewarding and enjoyable as well as the most memorable.

The skills and qualities you will develop are ones you will use in your working life. This unit should help prepare you effectively and practically to enter the world of leisure and recreation.

The success of this unit is down to you. You will not achieve the highest grades by reading a book and studying hard. Sensible study is always helpful but there are other qualities you will need to demonstrate:

- **Flexibility**
- **Sensitivity**
- **Discretion**
- **Objectivity**
- **Maturity**
- **Initiative**
- **Problem solving**
- **Conflict handling**
- **Time management**

There are limitless ways to complete this unit. There are endless choices for the central focus. You can base your project on any aspect of leisure and recreation; you can consider any aspect of your other five mandatory units or choose to apply an optional unit that interests you.

All projects, whatever their subject, will involve teamwork. Your team may contain 2 people or 50 people; you may even play a role in a large group but also form smaller groups to complete specific tasks.

The way your team is structured should be down to you and the other members. We will progress to that later on, meantime this unit can be as diverse as you want, as long as you achieve your objectives.

> This unit will progress through the aspects in the same order as your unit specifications. Use the information you have gathered from your other units and follow the link boxes scattered through the text.

Prefeasibility

This unit is about practical application, so let's begin by choosing something to do. Although the possibilities are endless, try to consider what subject area you

Links

Unit 1
Investigating leisure
and recreation
Unit 3
The sports industry
Unit 4
Marketing

would like to develop. It has to be related to leisure and tourism but that's the only condition. Here are some suggestions:

- **Organising a sports competition**
- **Running a playscheme**
- **Arranging an outdoor activities expedition**
- **Arranging a visit abroad, perhaps to coincide with a sports event**
- **Establishing a small business project**
- **Arranging a college or school party**
- **Organising the sports fixtures for your college or school**
- **Arranging a car boot sale**
- **Organising a summer activity programme**

You're now in the prefeasibility stage and you need to apply some common sense:

- **The project you choose must be complex enough to allow everyone to play an important role. It won't take much to plan a night out at a local theatre then a meal afterwards, so you won't get enough evidence for your portfolio. A week of entertainment, including catering, planning, varied programming of diverse activities, etc., allows much more flexibility and should also be more fun**
- **We may all have extravagant ideas for our projects but consider how much they will cost; it might be thrilling to plan a week's holiday in Barbados but it's unlikely that everyone could afford it. Perhaps compile a list to illustrate the extra challenges of a Caribbean holiday**
- **Seek advice from your teacher. They usually have lots of experience; they know what tends to work and what tends to fail. Besides that, they'll be happy to help you**

The number of students in your group will influence the way you choose your project. Perhaps a large group will split into smaller groups of two or three to prepare feasibility studies. Then all the groups will evaluate the feasibility studies and choose one project. A smaller group could choose a joint project and assess its suitability, amending the details after the feasibility study.

A project may be chosen for you and then you will have to prepare a feasibility study. For example, you are told you are going to arrange an outdoor activities expedition to northern Spain. You need to plan an itinerary and feasibility study for the expedition. Seek advice from your teacher.

On your own, consider what projects you would like to research for this unit. Now get together with your future team members and see if you have come up with the same or similar options.

Feasibility

Investigate your project's **feasibility** and present this in the form of a business plan. Here are some aspects you need to consider:

▼▼▼▼▼▼▼▼▼▼

Feasibility
practicality, viability, possibility

▲▲▲▲▲▲▲▲▲▲

- ✪ **Aims and objectives**
- ✪ **Customers and their needs**
- ✪ **Marketing**
- ✪ **Physical resource**
- ✪ **Financial aspects**
- ✪ **Staffing and teamwork**
- ✪ **Administration systems**
- ✪ **Timescales**
- ✪ **Legal aspects**
- ✪ **Contingency plans**
- ✪ **Review and evaluation**

Task
6.2

Compile a SWOT analysis of the activities or projects you may choose. This will help focus on the feasibility of your project.

Aims and objectives

Links

Unit 4
Marketing
Unit 5
Customer services

Aims and objectives should always be a central part of your project. Re-read them often to remind yourself what they are, to ensure you're focused on the job and to be certain you achieve them.

An aim is a general statement that specifies your overall target. For example, the aim of the Year 2 Leisure and Recreation Group is to successfully arrange a five-a-side indoor football league. You could even say your aim as a student is to successfully complete and achieve your Vocational A-level in Leisure and Recreation. An objective is more specific and may be given in greater detail. Here are some examples:

- **To attract 12 football teams to participate in a five-a-side indoor league**
- **To operate the five-a-side football league at a profit of £50**
- **To achieve a distinction in Vocational A-level Leisure and Recreation**

A good way to think about your aims and objectives is to write down all the aspects you want to achieve then draw up a statement that includes as many as possible. Finally specify all the other aspects in detail.

> Aims and objectives must be:
> - ★ Measurable
> - ★ With timescales
> - ★ Clear
> - ★ Achievable

Task 6.3

Prepare a set of aims and objectives for your project; make them clear and precise.

Customers and their needs

Link

Unit 5
Customer Service

The central focus of leisure and recreation is the customer. Depending on the project you have chosen the customers may be:

✪ **Children from a local school who attend a series of sports development sessions**

✪ **Other students in your school or college who take part in an end-of-year ball**

✪ **You and your friends on a week of outdoor activities in northern Spain**

Whoever the customers are, make sure you meet their needs. You will need to:

✪ **Identify these needs by gathering customer information through questionnaires, informal feedback, surveys and focus groups**

✪ **Meet these needs by acknowledging the information you have gathered**

It may be difficult to meet the needs of everyone. You may have to prioritise customer needs, identifying those that are essential and those that are desirable; be flexible. For instance, if a member of your group is diabetic, it may be that your project must include provision for self-catering and also diabetic catering. This is a customer need that must be met. If someone in your group cannot swim, you clearly cannot force them to do water sports during an expedition. You need to provide alternative arrangements.

Some customer needs are desirable; for example, the customer may stipulate a temperature of over 30°C. This is clearly desirable but it cannot be guaranteed. You will need to consider a compromise, perhaps offering alternatives. Instead of travelling abroad, maybe the customer can find their desired warmth at Center Parcs.

It's easy to lose sight of customer needs. If you're getting carried away with enthusiasm, stop and refocus. Here are some aspects to consider:

✪ **Customer care mission statement**

✪ **Customer care charter**

✪ **Identification of customers**

✪ **Customer satisfaction evaluation**

✪ **Recommendations for the future**

Task 6.4

Make a formal identification of the essential and desirable customer needs of the group. Develop these documents:

★ Customer care mission statement
★ Customer care charter
★ Identification of customers
★ Customer satisfaction evaluation
★ Recommendations for the future

Marketing

Link

Unit 4
Marketing

Some projects require more marketing than others. These projects will probably require a lot of marketing:

❂ **A trip to the theatre**
❂ **A fund-raising event**
❂ **A trip to a theme park**

However, most projects will benefit from a high profile and the creation of awareness. This may be through:

❂ **Sponsorship of your project by a local business**
❂ **A promotional campaign including advertising and public relations**
❂ **Fund-raising strategies that will also create awareness**

You have to match your product or service to your customers' needs then create awareness among your customers. Here are a few hints.

❂ **Seek sponsorship from businesses; write them letters explaining how they will benefit**
❂ **Try to do a joint promotion, e.g. a trip to Spain with First Choice booked in Going Places**

Task 6.5

Plan a relevant marketing campaign to maximise awareness of your project. Refer to Unit 4 if you need help.

Physical resources

All projects will require somewhere to meet, e.g. a room in a building, and basic equipment such as pens and paper. It is useful to identify these **physical resources** right at the start of the project then review them at regular intervals throughout.

> Most projects will require the following items:
> ★ Stationery, paper, pens, files
> ★ A base room with chairs and tables
> ★ A computer, perhaps a laptop
> ★ A first-aid kit
> ★ Telephone, email, etc.

Other physical resources will depend on the project. Here are some possibilities:

- ✪ **Canoes, paddles and spraydecks for outdoor activities**
- ✪ **Sports kit and trainers for a circuit training session**
- ✪ **Dishcloths, washing-up liquid and tea towels for a self-catering stay**
- ✪ **A field or car park for a car boot sale**

Try to be as specific as possible, stating types, quantities and any other relevant details:

Your swimming kit should include costume, goggles, hat and towel; it will be used twice daily.

You will need a canoe suitable for two with two life jackets, a throw line and a spraydeck suitable for two persons and two paddles.

Some physical resources may need to be assessed for suitability. This will include:

- ✪ **Appropriateness**
- ✪ **Location**
- ✪ **Proximity to customers**
- ✪ **Availability**
- ✪ **Value for money**
- ✪ **Accessibility**

Make sure a facility or venue is suitable for your chosen activity. If it is suitable, compare its price with some alternatives.

Task 6.6

★ Identify the physical resources needed to complete your project successfully

★ Assess the physical resources needed to complete your project successfully

Financial aspects

Link

Optional unit on business systems

All projects will require some sort of financial commitment. This is fairly straightforward but you do need to be thorough. Consider these aspects:

- ✪ **Simple budgeting**
- ✪ **The collection of monies**
- ✪ **The banking of monies**
- ✪ **Auditable procedures and processes**
- ✪ **Cash flow forecasts**
- ✪ **Financial contingency plans**

As a team you must consider the importance to place on money and financial procedures. The misuse of money and abuse of these procedures can lead to instant dismissal in the workplace. Treat financial matters with respect and account for everything you do.

Task 6.7

★ Set up relevant financial procedures

budgets

cash flow

petty cash

★ Establish a financial code of practice

★ Allocate money to budgets

★ Produce regular forecasts

★ Monitor all financial procedures

★ Consider the security of your finances

Staffing for teamwork

Link

Optional unit on human resources

There are several requirements you have to satisfy when generating evidence for your portfolio. Begin by asking yourself these questions then have a discussion with your teacher to make sure your portfolio will conform:

✪ **Is the project sufficiently complex to give each team member a worthwhile job?**

✪ **Will each team member have about the same amount of work through the year?**

✪ **What skills are needed to complete the task successfully?**

✪ **What skills are available within the team?**

✪ **Do the available skills match the required skills?**

The next thing to do is to have a look at recruitment:

✪ **Job analysis**

✪ **Job description**

✪ **Person specification**

✪ **Objective decision making**

✪ **Interviewing**

Then:

✪ **Training**

✪ **Appraisal**

And finally:

○ Organisational structure

The aim is to get the right person in the right job, so each student will need to:

○ Have a job description (using a standard format)
○ Receive regular training (through your teacher and your lessons)
○ Receive regular appraisals or reviews

You can allocate the jobs by taking it in turns to choose, or you can set up an interview panel that interviews candidates and appoints people to positions. Whichever method you adopt, you must maximise the group's strengths and minimise its weaknesses.

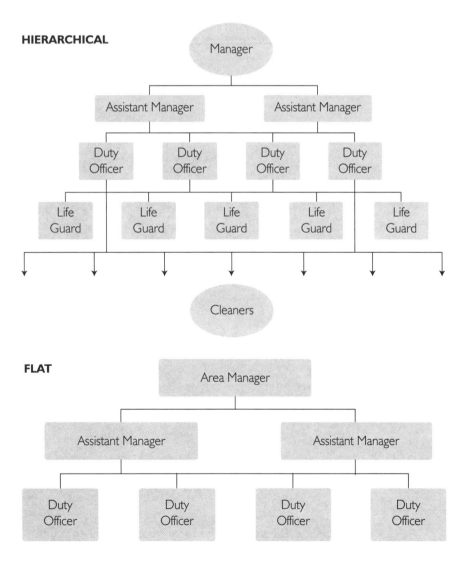

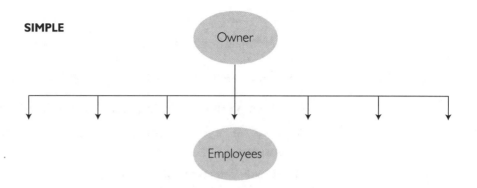

SIMPLE

Owner

Employees

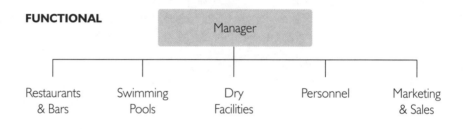

FUNCTIONAL

Manager

Restaurants & Bars | Swimming Pools | Dry Facilities | Personnel | Marketing & Sales

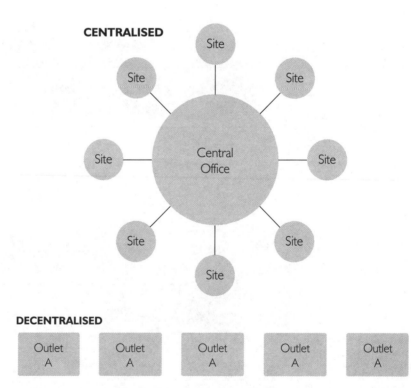

CENTRALISED

Site

Site

Site

Site

Central Office

Site

Site

Site

Site

DECENTRALISED

Outlet A | Outlet A | Outlet A | Outlet A | Outlet A

Different organisations have different structures

Each member of the group could complete a SWOT analysis on themselves and on each other. This could then be used to match the criteria on the person specification. Here are some aspects to consider:

- **Number of students in the group**
- **Time available**
- **Complexity of the project**
- **Human resources**

> Has the optional unit been covered?

You will also need to produce an organisational chart to represent your team. There are many ways to structure the team, but try to maximise efficiency, effectiveness and communication.

The leisure and recreation industry contains all types of organisation: hierarchical, flat, simple, functional, centralised, decentralised. The aim is to find a structure that will aid communication, allow quick decision making and help to motivate everyone. The jobs will depend on the project but here are some common ones:

- **Manager of the group (lecturer)**
- **A group coordinator or leader**
- **Vice group coordinator**
- **Financial controller**
- **Personnel coordinator**
- **Health, safety and security control**
- **Activities coordinator:**

> sport
>
> recreation

- **Fund-raising coordinator**

And some others:

- **Accommodation coordinator**
- **Catering coordinator**
- **Equipment coordinator**

Some jobs require more effort than others. As a group you must recognise this aspect and try to spread the load as evenly as possible. Consider whether shift work will even up people's responsibilities.

Link   **Page 257**

Optional unit on business systems

One of the most challenging aspects of working in a team is seeing your friends in a professional light. You must remain objective at all times and show that you understand there are tasks to complete and responsibilities to accept. If there are mistakes or failings, study the role, not the person.

Suppose the job of issuing receipts has not been successfully completed. You could say: 'Your job was to give out receipts when money was paid in and you did not'. Or you could say: 'Part of the responsibility of the role of financial coordinator is the issuing of receipts. This role has not been completed'. The first statement focuses on the person, the second on the job. It is useful to focus on the job as this helps minimise the confusion of personal and professional matters and it maintains objectivity.

It's quite a challenge to work together and make it a success. Try to be tolerant of each other and try to understand how conflicts may arise. Here are some golden rules:

- ✪ **Be honest**
- ✪ **Be precise**
- ✪ **Tackle problems**
- ✪ **Tolerate each other's weaknesses**
- ✪ **Don't bear grudges**
- ✪ **Accept constructive criticism**
- ✪ **Accept we all make mistakes**
- ✪ **Support each other**
- ✪ **Focus on the job not the person**
- ✪ **Leave your emotions at home**
- ✪ **Enjoy working with each other; it can be fun**

Task 6.8

★ Identify an organisational structure

★ Produce an appropriate organisational chart

★ Complete the recruitment process for the project

★ Establish a code of practice

behaviour

attendance

grievance

discipline

Administration systems

Link

Optional unit on business systems

Administration systems may be paper-based or IT-based (Table 6.1). All administration systems need to be:

○ **Accurate**

○ **Up to date**

○ **Easy to use**

○ **Accessible**

○ **Cost-effective**

Several factors will help you decide which system to use:

○ **How much the team knows about IT**

○ **The availability of IT to all the team**

○ **The number of students in your team**

It is likely that you will use both systems; the minutes and agendas of meetings are likely to be produced using information technology, but informal messages and notes may be written on paper and filed accordingly. Choose systems that increase the efficiency and effectiveness of the team.

Table 6.1   *Administration systems: IT versus paper*

	Advantages	*Disadvantages*
Information technology	Quick and easy Easy to update Cuts down on paper Secure storage Easy to email Accurate	Expensive Needs hardware Needs software Hardcopy backup
Paper	Easy to understand Cheap and accessible Little training	Easy to lose Hard to change Time-consuming High paper costs Prone to errors

Task 6.9

Decide on appropriate administration systems then put them into practice, monitoring and amending where necessary.

Timescales

By now you are probably well used to deadlines. Some people require deadlines to motivate them, others prefer to go at their own pace. In the workplace most jobs have some deadlines that have to be adhered to. A payroll is a good example; suppose you don't get paid because the payroll manager didn't fancy sticking to a deadline, you might feel rather aggrieved, and rightly so. This type of deadline is not negotiable. Other tasks have more flexibility and allow staff to choose their own sequence for completing them. The same will apply to your project. Here are some stages that are likely to have critical deadlines:

- ✪ **Choosing a place to visit**
- ✪ **Setting criteria for feasibility studies**
- ✪ **Presenting the feasibility studies**
- ✪ **Choosing from the feasibility studies**
- ✪ **Allocating jobs to people**
- ✪ **Booking accommodation and flights**
- ✪ **Paying for accommodation and flights**
- ✪ **Regular meetings**

Identify these key stages early on then agree a series of deadlines for the whole project. Communicate them to everyone and confirm they have been understood. Everyone in the team needs to be committed to the timescales and must understand the consequences of not meeting deadlines.

It is very easy to think that the odd day won't matter, but if this knocks back a key stage then the success of the whole project can be placed in doubt. For example, if one person does not pay for their air ticket on time, the project could be cancelled and everyone could lose their money.

The project leader will usually have the responsibility for ensuring any deadlines are met. This is arguably one of the most difficult aspects to achieve, but it will help if the deadlines have been agreed, identified, communicated, confirmed and reaffirmed.

Task 6.10

- ★ Identify and agree key stages and deadlines
- ★ Confirm key stages and deadlines
- ★ Monitor and amend key stages and deadlines

Legal aspects

Link

Unit 2
Safe working
practices

All projects will have legal obligations – things you will have to do under law. Even if the project is between you and your friends, there are certain items of legislation you should consider. Here are some of them:

- **Sex Discrimination Act**
- **Race Relations Act**
- **Equal Opportunities Act**
- **Health and Safety at Work Act**
- **Trade Descriptions Act**
- **Food Hygiene Regulations**
- **European Directives**

Quite often a certain role will specify responsibility for legal aspects, e.g. the health, safety and security coordinator. However, everyone has a responsibility to ensure all legal aspects are noted and your project demonstrates good practice. It may also be useful to carry out a risk assessment on the project. Consider these aspects:

- **Working in a hot climate may require sunscreen and drinks**
- **A sports festival will require first aid and emergency provision**
- **Food will require correct handling and storage**

It is impossible to provide an exhaustive list, but with the guidance of your teacher, you should be able to minimise the risk of an accident and avoid breaking any laws.

Task 6.11

★ Identify and assess hazards by completing a risk assessment for the project

★ Identify relevant legal obligations and ethical responsibilities for the project

★ Set up codes of practice to enforce them

Contingency plans

Link

Optional unit on running a leisure facility

One thing's for sure, nothing goes perfectly. If something can go wrong, chances are it will. Always consider the unexpected. Think about what would happen if things went wrong, particularly aspects you have no control over. Procedures for everyday occurrences are called normal operating procedures (NOPs). Procedures for unusual occurrences are called emergency operating procedures (EOPs). Contingency plans are also used in emergencies. Here are some contingencies to plan for:

- **The weather**
- **A power failure**
- **Sickness of staff**
- **Traffic delays**
- **Low turnout of customers**
- **Accidents**

A contingency plan will try to minimise the disruption if things do go wrong; this is achieved by putting a system on stand-by that can be called on quickly and effectively. Here are some examples:

- **Having stand-ins for key staff; stand-ins will be briefed and updated**
- **Having a generator on stand-by for electricity**
- **Having an indoor alternative if the weather is wet**

In the very worst circumstances, some events or projects may have to be cancelled. Sometimes it is impossible to prepare a contingency plan. Here are some examples:

- **An outdoor concert for 10 000 people may have to be cancelled if a thunderstorm becomes a health and safety risk**
- **An entire football team is ill with food poisoning and there are not enough substitutes**

Task 6.12

Establish a set of contingency plans allocated to each job, then identify and brief the people responsible

The cancellation of an event or project brings its own challenges. You may have to tackle bad publicity. As long as you follow the golden rules, you will have done the best you can. You cannot be held responsible for things beyond your control.

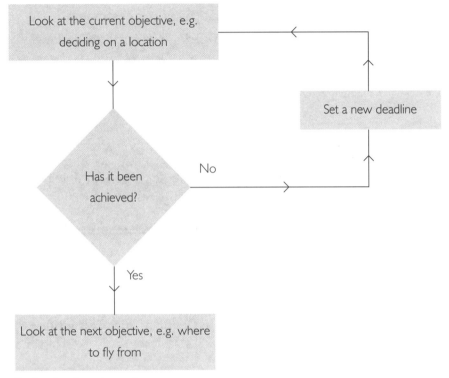

Evaluation is a dynamic process

- ✪ **Make a decision and stick to it**
- ✪ **Tell everyone who needs to know**
- ✪ **Be clear and keep the customer informed**
- ✪ **Be quick**
- ✪ **Be honest**
- ✪ **Give reasons**
- ✪ **Offer apologies**
- ✪ **Make quick and effective repayments**
- ✪ **Offer realistic alternatives**

Review and evaluation

Review and evaluate what you have done. When you draw up your timescale, built in opportunities for critical reflection. Assess what you have achieved and maybe revise your objectives and your timescale. This process is dynamic – it never stops. Page 249 describes how it works in more detail, but you can get a rough idea from the flow diagram on page 252. Once you have chosen a project, here are some aspects you could evaluate:

- ✪ **Are we meeting our deadlines?**
- ✪ **Are we meeting our objectives?**
- ✪ **Are we satisfying our customers?**
- ✪ **Are we meeting our legal obligations?**
- ✪ **What's our financial situation?**

Task 6.13

Using the key stages and deadlines you have agreed, complete the following evaluation:

- ★ Are we meeting our deadlines?
- ★ Are we meeting our objectives?
- ★ Are we satisfying our customers?
- ★ Are we meeting our legal obligations?
- ★ What's our financial situation?

Completing the feasibility study

The feasibility study takes a long time to complete. A successful project will thoroughly consider all the aspects we have covered here. When you've done a comprehensive feasibility study, you should present your findings as a business plan before you decide whether to go ahead.

Execution

Once you've decided to go ahead, that's when the work really begins. This is where you put things into action. By now you will have:

- ✪ **Identified your aims and objectives**
- ✪ **Identified tasks to be allocated**
- ✪ **Identified key stages in your timescale**
- ✪ **Identified a team structure**

Now you will have to:

- **Achieve these aims and objectives**
- **Allocate and complete the tasks successfully**
- **Stick to your deadlines**
- **Work within the team structure**

This needn't be difficult, but it may not be as easy as it sounds. Work systematically through your business plan and you should achieve your targets. Here are a few hints:

- **Remain focused on the aims and objectives of the project**
- **Concentrate on completing your job**
- **Remember you have team responsibilities**
- **Be loyal to your fellow team members**
- **Do not be afraid to use contingency plans**
- **If you need guidance then ask for help**
- **Acknowledge your mistakes and try to learn from them**
- **Deal with problems then move on; don't bear grudges**
- **Always be objective and try to stay positive**

The final part of the feasibility study mentions how the project will be reviewed and evaluated. It's quite common to work hard on a business plan that's realistic and viable. Preparation goes well and the event day arrives or the project nears completion. Avoid becoming complacent; don't sit back and breathe a sigh of relief. Persevere until everything is completed and all your evaluations are done:

- **Begin the big day with a briefing session; the team leader may:**
    give the team a pep talk
    confirm everyone's roles
    calm people's nerves
- **Ensure all team members are aware of emergency procedures**
- **Confirm timescales and any key stages of the project**
- **Emphasise the aims of the project**
- **Emphasise the importance of successful customer care**
- **Have a guaranteed method of contact; mobile phones are very useful**

> ★ Keep a logbook or diary throughout the project. This should state when, where and why you and your team were involved. Add your objective comments
>
> ★ Produce a group file that includes all minutes and agendas; keep it securely in a base room for access by the entire group

Evaluation

Everyone learns from their mistakes. It's certainly true of this unit. Given the chance to do some things again, you'll probably choose to do them differently. Looking back critically but constructively is known as evaluation. There are several reasons for evaluating a project:

- ✪ **To see whether it was a success**
- ✪ **To see whether customers were satisfied**
- ✪ **To identify its strengths and weaknesses**
- ✪ **To improve any future project**

Measurements

Measurable performance indicators will identify how successfully the human, physical and financial resources of a project have been used. They will measure this success using some of these variables:

- ✪ **Profit levels**
- ✪ **Total amount spent by each customer**
- ✪ **Staff costs**
- ✪ **Operating costs**
- ✪ **Number of visitors**

The results can then be compared with previous statistics for similar projects. More importantly, they can be compared with the aims and objectives of the project.

Opinions

Opinion is also a useful guide to success. Suppose you ask, Did you have a good time? Did you enjoy yourself? If the answer is yes, most people see this as value for money or, indeed, success. It is important to consider customers' opinions. But because they are subjective, they can be difficult to analyse. Here are some ways to gather opinions:

- **Surveys and questionnaires**
- **Informal feedback**
- **Focus groups**

Effective evaluation

An effective evaluation will use opinions and performance indicators. A good way of gathering feedback is to ask a series of questions:

- **Did we meet our objectives?**
- **Did we meet key deadlines?**
- **Did our planning promote effective performance?**
- **Was the project a success?**
- **What went well?**
- **What went badly?**
- **How well did the team work as a whole?**

When you answer these questions, you will need to consider your individual goas and the team's goals. And when you talk to your fellow team members about their performance, do it constructively by following these suggestions:

- **Be objective and stick to the facts**
- **Be honest and respectful**
- **Be assertive but sensitive**
- **Be prepared to accept criticism yourself**

Pass on your evaluations and comments to students in future years. Help them to capitalise on your strengths and help them to avoid some of your mistakes. We will now look at a case study where a group of students planned a week-long summer trip including sport and recreational activities.

The Malia Experience

A group of 17 second-year students studying a Vocational A-level in Leisure and Recreation decided they would plan a sports and recreation trip abroad. With the help of their teacher they considered the options available to them:

★ A camping trip

★ An outdoor activities expedition

★ A ski/winter sports trip

★ A hotel package 'holiday'

★ A self-catering break

★ An all-inclusive break

After discussing the complexity and other aspects of the project, the students decided on a self-catering break. They gave two reasons:

★ It allowed for flexibility in planning

catering

itinerary

★ It was relatively inexpensive

The students then drew up a list of criteria before embarking on their feasibility studies:

continued

continued

- ★ The project must take place during May
- ★ The project must take place during term time
- ★ The trip must be for one week
- ★ Each student pays no more than £350 plus spending money
- ★ The weather must be warm
- ★ The location must have activities for students
    - cultural
    - sporting
    - recreational
- ★ Fly to the destination from the nearest airport

As there were 17 students, they decided to split into small groups of 2 or 3. Each group then prepared a 10 minute presentation to cover the main parts of their feasibility study. The groups were randomly chosen to help students widen their 'friendship groups' before the teamwork later on. Each feasibility study followed the required format and each presentation covered the following items:

- ★ A short description of the location
- ★ A description of the accommodation, with pictures
- ★ Cultural, sporting and recreational activities
- ★ The total cost per student
    - travel
    - accommodation
    - tax and insurance
    - activities
- ★ The climate compared to the UK
- ★ The method and place of travel

A variety of locations were presented; they were then put into a grid (Table 6.2) for comparison. The presentations took place over two days so the students were still familiar

continued

continued

Table 6.2 *The Malia experience: a variety of locations were presented then put into a grid*

Criteria or destination	Cost	Climate	Activities	Accommodation rating	Airport

with all the details and could be confident in making their decisions.

When it came to the final choice, each student was allowed two votes: vote A for their first choice and vote B for their second choice. It all worked out quite clearly. Fifteen students chose Malia, Crete, as their first choice. Two students chose Cyprus, but their second choice was Crete so they were happy to go along with the majority. The choice was:

★   Emerald Apartments in Malia, Crete

★   Cost breakdown:

      travel   £187

      activities   60

      food   45

★   Fly from East Midlands Airport

★   Cultural visits to Knossos and Spinalonga

★   Plenty of water sports

★   Average expected temperature of 28°C

★   Dates: 14 May to 21 May

It was agreed this location would allow everyone to achieve their individual aims and objectives and the team to achieve its aims and objective. The students as a group then booked the trip with Kosma Holidays through their local travel agent. The deal included free insurance and a £10 deposit.

continued

continued

The next stage was to identify the team structure and the necessary jobs.

▶ ORGANISATIONAL STRUCTURE

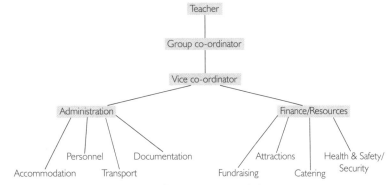

The organisational structure for the trip to Malia

Co-ordinators were identified for the following areas and job descriptions were drawn up. Only a few are included here.

- ★ Group coordinator/leader
- ★ Vice group coordinator/leader
- ★ Finance and resources
- ★ Catering
- ★ Accommodation
- ★ Fund-raising
- ★ Sport and recreation
- ★ Cultural activities
- ★ Personnel
- ★ Administration
- ★ Documentation
- ★ Health, safety and security

▶ ACCOMMODATION COORDINATOR

| Responsible to: | group coordinator |
| Responsible for: | people attending educational holiday |

continued

continued

Job objective: to choose or book accommodation and
flights to Crete for the whole group

Main duties and responsibilities

★ Choose accommodation with the group in Crete

★ Book the accommodation and flight to Crete

★ Get insurance that covers every single person in the
group

★ Arrange people into rooms in which they are happy

★ Sort out any problems with accommodation

★ Make sure people are looking after accommodation
while in Crete

► SPORT AND RECREATION COORDINATOR

Main duties and responsibilities

★ Organise and plan sporting attractions and events
for the group on its one-week educational trip

★ Choose sports suitable for the group:

water

land

spectator

★ Find chosen locations of sports and routes out and
back

★ Find out prices of the sporting events

★ Find out about insurance for the sporting activities

★ Write an itinerary for the week's activities

★ Work with other team members to plan activities in
full

continued

continued

▶ TRANSPORT COORDINATOR

Responsible to:	group coordinator
Responsible for:	people attending educational trip
Job objectives:	to arrange all transportation to Crete and on Crete

Main duties and responsibilities

★ choose transportation to and from East Midlands Airport

★ Arrange any special requirements, e.g. seating on the plane, vegetarian meals

★ Make sure transfers are included to and from the Emerald Apartments

★ Find out timetables and fares of local bus companies in Crete

★ Find out about other forms of transport available in Crete, with prices and timetables

The group set the following behaviour code:

While we are away, we will be expected to behave in an orderly fashion by taking the following guidelines into consideration:

★ Be aware of cultural differences; treat everyone with respect

★ Don't be argumentative with other people; aim to stay friendly with everyone

★ Tell someone where you're going at all times

★ Don't go anywhere on your own

★ Stick to deadlines and curfews

★ Don't bring back strangers to your rooms

★ Keep your room tidy and damage-free

★ Keep your key safe and hand it back when you depart

continued

continued

Every person did a SWOT analysis on themselves and then on each other; they identified the roles they preferred. The allocated roles were clear and there was no need to run any interviews to aid selection. The teacher verified the allocation of tasks to members of the group.

It was felt a weekly meeting was needed to discuss progress. It was set for Thursday afternoons, 2.30 till 3.30. A room was block booked for this purpose. It was also used as a base for the necessary documentation. The group coordinator chaired the meetings and the administration coordinator took minutes. A common format was agreed. Here are some other aspects to consider:

★ An agenda was distributed two days before each meeting

★ A nightly meeting was held once the project went ahead

★ The nightly meeting set actions for the next day

★ Two weeks before the trip, each student prepared a presentation

★ The presentations were led by the group coordinator

★ The presentations were watched by the students' supervisors

★ Each student explained their work so far and their role in Crete

★ After the presentations there was time for questions and answers

While they were in Crete, the students completed a 'mini' evaluation. Overall they thought the project ran smoothly and the week was a success, but here are the challenges they recorded:

★ Money: Students ran out of money. Money was unsecured in the accommodation. Collecting money was a problem

continued

continued

★ Attendance at meetings: Two students were identified as attending insufficiently. They were allocated additional tasks to balance out the workload. It was felt this would have been prevented by a code of conduct with disciplinary and grievance procedures.

★ Lack of information: The coordinators responsible for sports, recreation and culture struggled to gather information until they were in Crete

★ Illness: One member of the group fell ill and was hospitalised for two days. This prevented the health, safety and security co-ordinator taking part in one of the cultural activities

★ Uneven workload: The group leader was given time off and the vice group leader took over

★ Dehydration and sunburn: Some students had to be reminded of the strength of the sun and the dangers of a hot climate

★ Homesickness: Some students took time to settle down, missing home and friends

On their return to the UK the students then prepared an evaluation. As they had already produced a formal presentation immediately before the trip, this evaluation was more informal. It concentrated on:

★ The allocated role
★ The appropriateness of the team structure
★ The success of the project

This information was passed on to the first-year students who would be taking the unit next year.

Task 6.15

This is a factual account of a Vocational A-level project in Leisure and Recreation.

★ What is your impression of the project?

★ What are the strengths?

★ What are the weaknesses?

★ What would you do differently?

Useful websites in leisure and recreation

You will notice that throughout this book we have made reference to the value of the internet and various websites. The internet is excellent for learning about what happens in industry and the workplace, particularly in places where you would not be able to visit.

The information in these websites will not answer your Vocational A-level assessments but it will assist you in your investigations.

www.edexcel.org.uk	Edexcel
www.ocr.org.uk	OCR
www.qca.org.uk	Qualification Curriculum Authority
www.nike.com	Nike
www.english-heritage.org.uk	English Heritage
www.sprito.org.uk	National Training Organisation for Sport, Recreation and Allied Occupations
www.olympics.co.uk	British Olympics Association
www.lta.co.uk	The Lawn Tennis Association
www.ukathletics.co.uk	UK Athletics
www.english.sports.gov.uk	Sport England
www.ilam.col.uk	Institute of Leisure and Amenity Management
www.nt-education.org	The National Trust
www.sportsaid.org.uk	Sports Aid Foundation
www.bbc.co.uk	BBC
www.travelengland.org.uk	The English Tourist Board
www.virgin.col.uk	Virgin
www.thomson-holidays.com	Thomson Holidays
www.first-choice.com	First Choice
www.uksportscouncil.co.uk	UK Sport

Remember, websites change!

Glossary

Advertising a paid form of non-personal communication that aims to influence the customer in a particular way

Branding products with a set of common characteristics that make them distinctive from their rivals. This branding can be a logo, e.g. the Virgin logo. It can be colour identification, e.g. the purple chocolate wrapping of Cadbury. It can be music, e.g. the 'Eastenders' theme tune. Whatever it is, it has to be simple, short and instantly recognisable

Cinema licence premises where films, videos or live events are broadcast

Customer care policy tells the customer specifically what they can expect

Customer service ensuring the customer receives what they expect to receive

Hazard something that has the potential for harm

Empathy seeing something from someone else's viewpoint; treating someone the way you'd like to be treated yourself

External customers a customer who has no direct connection with an organisation and so visits it by choice

External factors influences that occur outside the organisation and that the organisation has little or no control over

Feasibility practicality, viability, possibility

Focus group a group of people who meet to exchange views and ideas

Indoor sports licence required if the operator is promoting sports events to which the public are invited

Informal feedback information gathered without any detailed plan or structure and often just by chatting to customers, both internal and external

Internal factors influences that occur inside the organisation and that can be controlled by the organisation

Internal customer a customer who has a direct working relationship with the organisation, most commonly a member of staff

Liquor licence for premises where alcohol is sold and consumed; can range from an on-licence through to an occasional licence; applications are made to the local magistrates' court

Marketing a management process responsible for identifying, anticipating and satisfying the requirements of the customer, profitably (Bruce Jewell, 1996, An Integrated Approach to Business Studies)

Marketing mix a collection of variables that an organisation can identify, manipulate and change to achieve a certain level of sales or targets

Marketing objective a statement that specifies what an organisation wants to achieve within a certain period of time, these statements are specific to marketing

Market segmentation is the process of grouping customers with a common interest or characteristic

Market research gathering information on the needs and desires of the customer, the product or service, or a related subject

Mission statement a broad declaration that tells the customer what to expect

Mystery shopper someone who visits a facility on behalf of its owner to assess the customer service without the staff knowing

Non-verbal communication a method of communicating without words or voice

Partnership owned and run with between 2 and 20 people; decision making is shared; all partners are liable for debts incurred by the business

Physical resources generally buildings and equipment, they are tangible products you can see and touch

Private Limited Company owners enjoy limited liability, i.e. they are only liable up to the amount they have invested in the company; the abbreviation 'Ltd' appears after the organisation's name; shares are not offered on the stock exchange but accounts must be published annually

Product the actual item or service that is on sale; the thing the customer will buy or experience

Product life cycle the stages in a product's life

Public entertainment licence for premises where any form of public entertainment takes place; issued through a local authority

Public Limited Company known as PLCs; investors again share the benefit of limited liability; accounts must be published annually

Risk the likelihood of the harm occurring and the severity of its consequences

Sole trader owned and run by one person; they have personal control over all aspects of the business but are personally liable for any debts incurred by the business

Successful customer service ensuring the customer receives what they expect, plus a little bit more

Survey a structured and planned method of gathering information, often using a series of specific questions

Index